Freight Broker Business Startup

Step-by-Step Guide to Start, Grow and Run Your Own Freight Brokerage Business in as Little as 30 Days

Clement Harrison

© **Copyright 2020 - All rights reserved.**

The content contained within this book may not be reproduced, duplicated or transmitted without direct written permission from the author or the publisher.

Under no circumstances will any blame or legal responsibility be held against the publisher, or author, for any damages, reparation, or monetary loss due to the information contained within this book, either directly or indirectly.

<u>Legal Notice:</u>

This book is copyright protected. It is only for personal use. You cannot amend, distribute, sell, use, quote or paraphrase any part, or the content within this book, without the consent of the author or publisher.

<u>Disclaimer Notice:</u>

Please note the information contained within this document is for educational and entertainment purposes only. All effort has been executed to present accurate, up to date, reliable, complete information. No warranties of any kind are declared or implied. Readers acknowledge that the author is not engaged in the rendering of legal, financial, medical or professional advice. The content within this book has been derived from various sources. Please consult a licensed professional before attempting any techniques outlined in this book.

By reading this document, the reader agrees that under no circumstances is the author responsible for any losses, direct or indirect, that are incurred as a result of the use of the information contained within this document, including, but not limited to, errors, omissions, or inaccuracies.

Table of Contents

Introduction 2

Chapter 1 A Freight Broker—The World's Most Sought After Middle Man 8

    Role of a Freight Broker 12

    Shippers and Carriers 15

    Freight Broker Duties 17

    How Will I Make Money? 20

Chapter 2 Is It Worth It? 24

    Growth Projections 27

    Technological Disruption 29

    Competitive Advantage 30

Chapter 3 The Importance of Knowing Your Target Market 35

    Niche (Micro) Marketing 36

    Benefits of Niche Marketing 36

    Possible Challenges in Niche Marketing 40

    How to Choose a Niche 42

    Is it possible to have more than one niche? 48

Chapter 4 Let's Talk About Money 52

    Start-up Costs 52

    The Profit 59

The Pricing.. 65

Chapter 5 Writing a Business Plan 68

   Value and Importance of Having a Business Plan 69

   Types of Business Plans 74

   Lean Business Plan 77

   Freight Broker Business Plan Template 83

Chapter 6 How to Find Carriers and Shippers 90

   What Do Customers Look For? 98

   Creating Quality Brokerage Business 103

Chapter 7 The Legalities and Formalities 109

   Sole Proprietorship 110

   Partnerships 111

   Corporations 113

   S Corporations 114

   Limited Liability Company (LLC) 116

   Registering Your Business 117

   Compliance Requirements 119

   The Transportation Management System (TMS) 122

   Benefits of Freight Broker Software 123

   Choosing the Best Software 125

   Top Freight Brokerage Software 128

Chapter 8 Grow Your Business With Smart Marketing 135

- Originality 137
- Customer-Centric Content 138
- Online Marketing 138
- Understand Customer Needs 140
- Create a Professional Website 141
- Work on Your Content Strategy 142
- Market Your Strengths 143
- Buyer Journey Stages 144
- Call to Action (CTA) 145
- Quality Landing Pages 146
- Perform A/B Testing 146
- Cold Calling 147

Conclusion 153
References 159

Introduction

"A small business is an amazing way to serve and leave an impact on the world you live in."

Nicole Snow

Every morning, we wake up to the news of entrepreneurs making huge strides in the world of business. As much as their success can be attributed to their efforts, have you ever wondered how all these businesses come to thrive? Beyond the technical or professional aspects of their operations, almost all businesses depend on some deliveries. Look at companies like Amazon that have revolutionized the transport and logistics industry. They ship almost anything you can think of under the sun. In a world as interconnected as ours, freight transport and logistics are among the most crucial business entities in the world, responsible for the success stories you read about in the news. Unfortunately, they never get the acclamations.

Take a moment and think of a world without the freight industry. Imagine the challenges we would go through, struggling to get cargo from one point to the other. It's unfathomable. The freight transport industry is vast, and there is enough space for you in it, too. Starting and running a freight brokerage business is not an easy task. For someone new to the industry, it might sound like an insurmountable task.

Even those who have worked in the industry for years might not be able to wrap their heads around taking that leap of faith and starting their own brokerage business. This guide will help you to start and run a freight brokerage business.

Regardless of your experience in the industry, the requirements, rules and legal obligations in the industry are clear. Using this book, you are well on your way to learning how to prepare yourself for the business, drawing up a business plan, researching the market and even carving out a niche for yourself.

The job prospects and outlook for freight brokers is exciting today. It is one of the fastest-growing sectors in the transport industry. Online shopping has made it easier for people to purchase virtually anything they want regardless of where it is located and that is one of the reasons for the steady growth in the freight industry. This points to one thing—there is a demand for freight brokers.

Shippers need carriers to move cargo from one point to the next. However, it is difficult for most shippers to coordinate with carriers. This is where you come in. You are the liaison between the shipper and carrier, and in the process, you earn a tidy sum for your effort. Freight brokerage offers you a lot of flexibility and independence such that you can become your own person. You can run the business on your own and bring one or a few more people to assist as your business grows.

You don't even need a physical office to start. Many freight brokers leverage their businesses by working from home and, using some of the best software in the market, coordinate cargo movement with carriers to the shipper's destination. If you are the kind of person who doesn't like someone breathing down their neck, this is something you should think about.

The freight industry has so much potential for growth. I have seen many young entrepreneurs start from scratch and, in a few years, grow their brokerage businesses into large companies, hiring agents to work under them.

The door to personal and business success opens to anyone who is bold enough to pursue their dreams. You have to be passionate about what you set your mind to. By all means, I have enjoyed all manner of success because I took a chance and invested in my financial future. When you don't come from generational wealth, you have to put in the work, at times harder than everyone else. That is the grit that helped me to succeed in life.

Freight brokerage is an incredible business opportunity. One of the reasons I love this particular venture is the kind of people you meet all the time. With all manner of cargo passing through your hands, you rub shoulders with companies and individuals you might never have imagined meeting, but that's beside the point.

My vision while writing this book was to give you the best introduction to the freight brokerage business. I realize that you might be at a different point in life than the next individual, so the challenge was getting everyone on the same page. Whether or not you have experience in the freight industry, you will find this book useful. You will learn, among other things, how to find shippers and carriers, instructions on the brokerage license, marketing techniques to make your brand visible, and how to choose the right business structure within which you will operate the business.

This book is organized so that you can use it as a guide in every step of your brokerage business. You will learn not only how to start the business but also how to find clients. Speaking of clients, one of the common fears I have come across in the freight brokerage industry is that the market is saturated, making it difficult for them to set out on their own. This is nothing but fear of the unknown, which happens to the best of us, and is normal in business. As much as the freight industry is saturated, new customers are coming into the market every other day. The industry has grown over the years, and with growth comes the need for specialization, diversification and other disruptive approaches. You can be a part of this new dynamic. I included an industry forecast to show you how good the prospects are, which is why you need to overcome the defeatist mentality that the market is saturated.

For most entrepreneurs, just getting into the business and facing the reality of writing a business plan is another stumbling block. I realized that many people had never written a business plan, and that is also okay. I mean, you probably never imagined you'd find yourself building a business from scratch, right? You will learn how to write a business plan and the importance of one.

The freight business is a relationship business. You need connections to make it in this industry. Even if you don't know anyone, let your business acumen do the talking for you. Network, join discussion forums, talk to former colleagues, do everything you can to get your business name on people's lips. Build relationships with carriers and shippers, and more importantly, be efficient, and you will run a successful freight brokerage business.

From my experience in this industry, freight brokerage is not for the weak. You must be a passionate, result-driven fellow to cut it in this industry. Your attitude and motivation will be key to your success in freight brokerage.

Chapter 1
A Freight Broker—The World's Most Sought After Middle Man

Logistics is one of the most critical departments in a business and the unsung hero in many success stories. Every other day you see companies posting impressive performance reports at the close of their financial year, and most of these are attributed to their sales and marketing efforts. Take a moment and think about it, where would companies like Amazon be without an efficient logistics network? You can market all you want, spend so much money on advertising, offer promotions, giveaways and all manner of offers to entice customers. But behind the scenes, an inefficient logistics network will render your efforts null and void. I mean, what's the point of promoting your business if you cannot deliver on time, and that's if you deliver at all, right?

Freight brokerage is an essential part of the logistics business. Do I really need to use a freight broker? This is a common question in shipper circles. To answer this question, let's understand what a freight broker does. A freight broker is someone who organizes the smooth movement of consignments between shippers and carriers. For making this movement smooth, they receive a commission. Essentially, without a freight broker, the shipper-carrier engagement is often marred with several inconveniences and mishaps. Freight brokers, therefore, bring a vital element to shippers and carriers—value addition.

Over the years, businesses have grown through specialization—focusing on the things they are good at and outsourcing the rest to experts. By focusing on their core business, entities can leave things like logistics to freight brokers because that is their specialty. Through freight brokers, value addition is realized by increased efficiency and flexibility in moving items through the supply chain from the originator to the end-user. Unless their core business is shipping, many businesses today use freight brokers for shipping and logistics. Here's an interesting fact: More than 80% of Fortune 500 companies use freight brokers and other third-party firms to handle services that are not primarily in their purview.

Looking at this scenario, you must understand your role in the supply chain when you venture out as a freight broker. Customers need value, which you will offer through your experience, expertise and connections in the industry. This is not a coincidence either, because it is essentially a cause-and-effect relationship. The money saved by your clients on shipping improves their business model, helping them scale their operations. As they grow, their business volume under your docket grows, so you grow too.

Freight brokerage is such a close-knit industry that if you don't add value to the customer, they will always look to get better services elsewhere. So, in your capacity, the following are some benefits you must bring to the table or face extinction:

1. **Scalability and flexibility**

As businesses evolve through different cycles, you prop them up through your brokerage services. This way, you offer your business partners less or more capacity as and when their business needs arise. This is important because, among others, you eliminate the challenge of seasonality in some industries.

In the long run, you offer businesses an opportunity to save money, time and other resources, which they can then divert towards strengthening the core functions of their operations. You essentially provide businesses a dedicated shipping and logistics department without them incurring the cost of setting up and running it on their own. In terms of the weight off their shoulders, think of training, auditing, invoices, repair and maintenance, staffing and the associated costs. You are that strategic partner every business needs.

2. **Professionalism**

Business partners come to you for the one thing you are good at—shipping. By all means, make sure you are good at it. By working with you, they leverage their business on your knowledge, experience and grasp the industry's best practices. This, coupled with access to the latest technology in the industry, helps you to offer them the level of service they would appreciate.

One thing you should never take for granted in this industry is networking. The freight brokerage business is one where connections matter more than what you know. From your networks, customers hope to benefit from volume discounts, capacity handling, and any other service that would make working with you better than the prospect of running an internal shipping department.

3. **Partnership**

When you start working with shippers and carriers, you become a strategic partner. This is not a one-off business venture. Since you essentially work for the customers, you must prioritize their needs and interests. Look at it this way, if they succeed, you succeed. If their business grows, yours grows. This is the kind of mutually beneficial partnership that you should strive to achieve.

Role of a Freight Broker

Having seen what you bring to the table, what is your role in this industry? You are the most in-demand middleman in the world of business. Primarily, your work is to help shippers and carriers. You connect shippers with carriers who are qualified and ready to transport their cargo. Once you broker a deal between the shipper and carrier, you facilitate the movement of their load until it gets to the intended destination. This means that you need to keep an open line of communication between the shipper and carrier throughout the process. You might not be a carrier or shipper, but you play an important role in cargo movement as a transport intermediary.

Regardless of the size of your operation, there are some tenets that you must follow if you are to succeed in the industry. As we discuss them below, you will realize that they are all related. Together, they will help you cultivate an environment where your brokerage business can grow and offer shippers and carriers quality services.

1. **Ensure freight is insured**

One of your responsibilities is to ensure that all cargo you handle has appropriate insurance coverage and that the selected carriers also have relevant liability coverage. When handling cargo, your shipper must disclose the value of the cargo. This helps determine the liability cover value, which is usually determined by factors like the type of commodity, value, class and so on.

2. **Carrier selection**

This might sound obvious, but it is important to ensure that you offer your customers quality services. There are many carriers in the industry, but not all are always suitable for the task. You must understand the shipper's needs, and where applicable, the specific needs of their cargo; hence, finding an appropriate carrier.

For example, most carriers' average load height is 96". In case your shipper's load is 100", you have to rethink the conventional delivery method. Perhaps a flatbed would be better than a regular truck, to make loading easier, in this case. You could also consider a trailer with swing doors, making it easier to load the cargo. This is why understanding the customer's freight and their needs is important. You can be certain that if you pull this off without a hitch, you will be the go-to broker for that shipper's business. Where possible, advise the shipper on all the options available to them.

3. **Instruct carriers**

One of the common documents you will use is a bill of lading. In this document, you provide all the information necessary about the cargo to the carrier. For example, perhaps the delivery is to a residential area, maybe the shipper expects a call before delivery to make special arrangements, and so on. You must convey all the instructions requested by the shipper to the carrier, even if they seem unorthodox.

Most shippers will be upfront with you if there are special instructions or requests to go with their cargo. It is only fair that you do the same with carriers, so there are no surprises when delivering the cargo.

4. **Check carrier safety ratings**

Always vet carriers, and know their safety and liability ratings. Carriers run into unavoidable problems on the road from time to time, so it is wise to ensure their ratings are within an acceptable score range.

Given the industry's competition, some carriers offer ludicrous prices that are too good to be true. Note that some carriers offer incredibly low prices as they cannot compete with qualified competitors at the same price because of low safety and liability scores. Many freight brokers have fallen prey to the allure of cheap freight, only to suffer losses in the long run. Each time you assign a shipper's cargo to a carrier, your reputation is on the line until the shipment arrives at the intended destination and in the expected condition.

There are many qualified carriers out there, and it is your duty to find them, know their rates and ensure that the shipper's freight arrives safely and efficiently. At the moment, identity theft has crept into the industry, so you must be careful when vetting carriers.

Organized crime rings have drivers whose safety ratings check out, but they use fake motor carrier numbers to steal consignments in the real sense. This is also a good reason to ensure your business.

5. **Cost reduction**

Everyone worries about costs when running a business. In particular, shippers are more concerned about costs because it eventually influences the price at which they can conduct business and break even. Cost reduction is one of the reasons why shippers look for freight brokers. Making a profit in any business is about thin margins, and this is where you come in.

Shippers rely on your experience and connections to streamline their supply chain, and in the process, find ways of reducing the logistics costs compared to what they would spend if they moved cargo on their own. Besides, you are a consultant, so the shipper does not need an in-house freight handling department with employees, saving them more money in the process.

Shippers and Carriers

In freight logistics, a carrier is an individual or company with the legal obligation of transporting cargo on water, land or air. Carriers work with shippers to move stuff from one place to the next. There are two types of carriers in the market: contract carriers and common carriers.

Contract carriers refer to the individuals or companies that offer transport services for a shipper, but on a long term arrangement. The contract carrier and the shipper sign a contract whereby they work together for a predetermined period and under specific conditions.

On the other hand, common carriers are individual or company transport providers who offer carrier services to anyone or any company. They must be licensed to offer their services. Since they are not bound by contract to a specific shipper, common carriers can work with as many shippers as they can handle within the day.

Another term that you will come across in the industry is a global freight forwarder. This is a carrier that handles shipments from one country to the other. Some carriers are contractually bound to operate only within the country, offering interstate transport and logistics services.

In terms of the delivery services, carriers offer different modes of transport. As a freight broker, it is always advisable to look for carriers who provide multiple transportation modes. This gives you a lot of options when moving a customer's cargo. Ideally, the decision on how to transport the shipper's cargo usually depends on their express instructions, the costs involved, and the cargo's nature.

There are several authority organizations to which freight carriers should be registered. They oversee operations within the transportation industry and set standard rules of engagement and practices under which cargo is moved. As a freight broker, you should know about the governing bodies in your industry so that, when vetting carriers, you choose only those who are duly licensed. Note that the carrier you choose will be responsible for transporting goods worth millions of dollars for your shipper customers. Therefore, you must exercise due diligence in this regard. Besides, your reputation is on the line, so ensure that you choose carriers who share the same business growth values as you do.

Shippers are individuals or businesses that own or supply the cargo being transported by the carrier. Shippers are also known as consignors.

Freight Broker Duties

One of the realities of life as an intermediary is that your duties are always diverse. Given that you are running the business on your own, for example, you might not be in a position to delegate tasks. Unless you start your brokerage business with a team to help from time to time, all the work involved in the brokerage business is on you. Let's have a look at some of the tasks you will have to do:

Logistics Operations

Well, this is a logistics-based business, so you must be prepared for this. If you have been in the brokerage industry before, you have some knowledge of some of the logistics tasks you will perform. Even if you are new to the industry, a broker's logistics duties are things you can manage and get used to easily. Here are some of your duties:

- Coordinating and planning delivery and pick-up schedules between carriers and shippers
- Managing dispatch schedules
- Monitoring and updating real-time shipment statuses to customers
- Efficiently organize multiple deliveries
- Improve the business through innovative sales strategies
- Mediate and resolve freight inconsistencies and challenges

Marketing and Communication

Your business must be visible if you are to make money in this industry. For that to happen, you will have to invest in a proper marketing campaign. There are many marketing tools and resources you can use to make this happen. Here are some of your duties:

- Constant communication with shippers to update them on the delivery progress

- Networking and maintaining positive relationships with relevant stakeholders
- Discussing and negotiating price agreements with different carriers
- Reach out to current and former shippers and carriers for new business
- Lead generation
- Building and reviewing the sales pipeline

Later in this book, we will discuss in-depth how to market your brokerage firm, including successful strategies that have been used by brokers over the years.

Maintaining paperwork

It is your legal obligation as a freight broker to process and maintain paperwork for all the transactions. For compliance purposes, you are expected to maintain paperwork for transactions for at least three years, during which shippers and carriers can go through and verify the information for whichever purpose.

Besides the legal requirements, you must also ascertain that all the freight paperwork involving transactions under your brokerage firm are duly filed and approved before you engage carriers for transportation services.

How Will I Make Money?

The logistics industry is one of the wealthiest, with billions of dollars in cargo value being transported daily. It is also an industry with many players, from shippers, carriers, brokers and other agents, all of who share in the pie. Before you start your brokerage firm, you definitely want to know how you will get paid for your effort.

As an intermediary, most of your work is no different from a salesman. However, the difference is that freight brokers are generally paid based on the gross load margin instead of the gross revenues. This is because, in this industry, gross revenues are not considered as the underlying metrics. Profits in freight brokerage are realized as a function of each buy or sell transaction that you make. To understand this, we must consider the relationship between gross margins and gross revenue.

Gross revenue in this industry is the earnings you make from charges levied to shippers (your customers). The difference between your charges to shippers and what you pay carriers is the gross margin. We can represent this in a simple equation as follows:

Gross margin = Price charged to shipper – Price paid to carriers

The difference you get from this equation represents the real value of profitability for each transaction.

Note that the distinction between these two charges is important in freight brokerage just as much as it is in determining your brokerage commission.

The last thing you want to do is address your earnings as a function of gross revenues. This can be so deceptive and will never give you the true picture. The freight brokerage industry is different from other industries because in those industries, the cost of manufacturing or services rendered is usually stable, albeit relatively. On the other hand, the cost of hiring carriers is determined by a lot of factors, most of which change all the time. Let's use an example to explain this further:

$10,000 charged to shipper – $9,000 paid to the carrier = $1000 gross margin or net revenue

$4,000 charged to shipper – $3,000 paid to the carrier = $1000 gross margin or net revenue

If you look at the figures above, the gross revenue is higher in the $10,000 load, but in the real sense, each of the loads brings in the same gross margin.

Another term that is used to describe gross margins is net revenue. In accounting and finance terms, net is usually the term used to determine the profits you retain after making all allowable deductions, in this case, what you collect from shippers once you pay carriers to move the cargo to their destination.

The other difference between the freight brokerage industry and other industries, especially those where tangible goods are produced, is that the freight industry's transportation cost is often volatile. Because of this, the role of a freight broker is more or less similar to a financial broker. You buy and sell assets based on the prevailing market conditions and earn a commission for the services rendered.

This is the same model that is employed by most online retail platforms like eBay. As much as billions of dollars are transacted on their platforms, they earn a commission on each transaction value. Therefore, their commissions are their net revenues after accounting for payroll costs, administrative, marketing, technology and any other functions.

Whether you sell $400,000 or $40,000 to shippers in freight brokerage, this is immaterial to determining your commissions earned. Besides, commissions and compensation vary from one broker to the next. Since every broker can set their rates according to their business model and other considerations, there is no universal commission plan. Depending on how your brokerage business works, some brokers earn a base salary and commissions, while others are only paid on commission as a gross margin of loads.

Chapter 2
Is It Worth It?

Going into any business, one of the common doubts people usually have is whether they are making the right choice. Granted, you are investing a lot of money, probably most of your savings into the business, so it is only fair that you should know your investment will be safe. In light of the recent coronavirus pandemic, many people have held back on investments, and for a good reason. If you heed financial advisors and analysts' advice, you must be prudent in your investments as we advance.

What does this mean for the freight brokerage market? Regardless of their opinions, most analysts and experts on freight and logistics believe that as much as 2020 was a year full of uncertainties, the freight industry was shaken up like every other industry, but for its resilience, it has grown and will keep growing over the next couple of years.

There are many reasons for the sustained growth in this industry. One of these is the continued growth of online retail. With more businesses operating online, many people operate the back end side of their businesses from warehouses. They market and engage customers online, but goods are delivered from their warehouses to the customer. If you expand on this to the context of interstate and international trade, you can begin to understand why the freight industry keeps growing and the prospect for freight brokers.

Coming into the year 2020, North America was the biggest freight brokerage market, and this trend is widely expected to persist over the coming years. Other brokerage markets of interest include Canada and Mexico.

As the industry's middle man, your role is to link trucking companies and shippers with customers. As the industry grows, systemic challenges further shift attention to freight brokers' role. One of these is the shortage of truck drivers in the market. In light of the pandemic, many truck drivers have been unable to carry out their duties. The shortage of drivers meant that brokers had to increase the cost of getting goods to shippers as demand increased for the few truck drivers available.

On their end, it is only natural for shippers to find more affordable brokers whose pricing is within an acceptable range. An interesting feature of the freight brokerage market is that it usually feels changes in other related industries. For example, as the e-commerce world grows, so does the need for long-distance freight delivery.

When companies like Amazon launch their brokerage service, you know the market is ripe for exponential growth. The value proposition for Amazon freight brokerage, for example, is that shippers can easily get quotes and match with a carrier right away. Their entry into the digital brokerage service matches customers' demand for shipping with the available trucking capacity. With other digital competitors, like Transfix, Convoy and Uber Freight, already in the industry, this is proof that there is room for anyone who can offer value to the customers.

Amazon uses their wealth in artificial intelligence to match available freight needs and trucker capacity, such that in the long run, customers enjoy cost savings and efficiency. It is not just about the large freight shipments. Amazon has also expanded its capacity to deliver smaller packages, offering last-mile delivery to its customers.

Now, suppose you consider the fact that Amazon has quite the experience in delivering shipments all over the world. In that case, their entry into the brokerage market gives them an edge over not so innovative brokers. Their operation's sheer size puts them at an advantage because they can offer highly competitive prices and, more importantly, a streamlined freight delivery service.

So, is it still worth it, investing in freight brokerage, to compete with giants like Amazon? Yes, it is. You might not be able to compete with them muscle-for-muscle, but you can learn from their approach, innovate and offer incredible value to your customers. Indeed, large brokers can offer excellent prices, but their size comes with unique challenges that could have been avoided by using a relatively smaller broker. For example, how many times have you heard people complaining about losing one or a few of their packages that should have arrived from Amazon? Large companies can offer so much, but simple things like these make some customers shy away from them and prefer smaller brokers who can give them the best services and listen to their concerns.

Growth Projections

The freight market is a highly fragmented industry, and for this reason, players in the market must come up with different growth approaches. Over the years, participants in the market have had to leverage drivers like demand for transport and logistics services to spur growth opportunities in the market. With more opportunities for growth and the impact of the global pandemic, everyone involved in the freight industry, including carriers, shippers and brokers, has to focus on a growth prospect in a fast-growth market while at the same time cementing their position in the slow-growth segments.

Increased activity in the manufacturing sector raised more risks and complexities in the supply chain. Due to this, many industries have since realized the benefit of working with freight brokers to streamline goods' transportation. In this capacity, brokers essentially design, manage and optimize the distribution network to ensure that goods are delivered on time from the source to the destination and in good condition. For the end-users, this translates to reduced operational costs.

As the demand for transport and logistics services increases from most of the end-user industries like e-commerce, manufacturing, pharmaceutical, auto and FMCG, it is expected that the demand for freight brokerage will increase in equal measure, with a compounded annual growth rate of at least 4% in the period up to 2024.

Another possible reason for growing demand is the increase in low-cost manufacturing products from countries like Mexico, Brazil, China and South Africa. It is widely expected that this will further increase demand for freight brokerage in North America, given that the products from these countries have favorable markets in the US.

In particular, growth in the e-commerce sector is one factor that has led to an increase in the less than load (LTL) freight market. LTL refers to the transportation of small cargo that does not warrant a full truckload. Shippers generally consolidate a lot of LTL cargo in one truck and have them transported to different destinations. In this case, a freight broker's role is to organize and plan the delivery route for the carrier, in the process fully maximizing the capacity of that truck. Through LTL freight, you minimize shipping costs and reduce carbon emissions, which many players in the industry currently value.

Technological Disruption

Technology is bound to play an essential role in the growth of the freight brokerage industry. From what we have seen in the past, everyone in the industry is looking at integrating some aspect of disruptive technology into their business. In particular, shippers are in a good position to optimize their shipping schedules and reduce costs in the process. On the other hand, carriers make the most use of their haulage assets.

Tech companies are also making their mark in the industry. Take Uber Technologies, for example. Since the launch of Uber Freight in 2017, more than 400,000 drivers across 36,000 carriers have been contracted on the app, serving thousands of shippers' needs. Other companies that have joined the fray include Convoy, Transfix and Loadsmart. Each of these companies has invested in algorithms that help shippers find carriers to transport their loads efficiently.

Of course, this is one of those tech disruptions that will challenge traditional brokerage firms. What you need to do is to embrace technology and stay relevant in the market. No one likes delays when it comes to transport and logistics, so the best move for you would be to align yourself with such technological advancements.

Apart from the tech giants entering the market, even traditional brokers in the industry have embraced technology in one way or the other. To remain competitive and relevant in the market, carriers have also picked up on the trend and adapted them into their operations. This tells you that, apart from learning about the freight brokerage's ins and outs, you also need to learn about the tech aspect so that you have a clear path laid out by the time you go in.

Competitive Advantage

The transportation management industry is currently enjoying a competitive advantage in light of increased tech disruption. This can be seen in freight brokerage markets and third-party logistics sectors. While tech can be seen as a disruptor, it has also leveled the playing field for brokers. For small and medium-sized brokers, the technological disruption is a welcome advancement because it allows them to stay competitive in the market, notwithstanding large brokerage firms' efforts.

Technology plays a vital role in brokerage. First, it helps with visibility and allows brokers to use freight matching to cover more loads efficiently. This is something that small brokers have struggled with over the years compared to more prominent brokers. The automation process improves your effectiveness such that you can now handle more business than you would with a manual system.

Another area where technology has assisted small brokers is shipment visibility. This means that your customers are now in an excellent position to know more about their shipment remotely. This means you no longer have to keep calling them with updates. Real-time shipment tracking has made work easier for brokers and given shippers peace of mind. On the part of the carriers, they are fully aware of the role technology plays throughout the haulage period, so they strive to make deliveries on schedule. Such changes free up more time for you to spend on managing your business, marketing, focusing on growth, networking and any other aspect of your business, thereby leveling the playing field and allowing you to grow just as fast as larger brokers.

Finally, one of the areas where tech brings a competitive advantage is automated invoicing. Forget about the days of manual invoicing where a lot of time and energy would be lost. Automated invoicing increases efficiency and has also reduced the lag between cargo delivery and payment, which traditionally made business difficult for many small brokers. As long as you were not getting your invoices paid on time, you would end up with piling and expensive debt, and in the long run, shutting down was the best option since small brokers did not have the financial muscle that larger brokers had in the industry.

Essentially, by leveling the playing field for small and large brokers alike, the competitive advantage is a win-win situation for everyone. Back in the day, shippers had a difficult time trusting small brokers. There was the concern that a broker can wake up one day and close their operation for lack of funds. Today, however, automated invoicing means that brokers get paid on time and can handle most shippers' business regardless of their size. Besides, through LTL freight, many shippers embrace the concept of consolidation, significantly reducing the cost of delivery to their destinations. It is safe to say that the technological disruption has fostered trust between shippers, freight brokers and carriers.

Going forward, you must have a clear vision of what to do and how to go about starting your brokerage firm. You need to know how to set competitive prices and, more importantly, how to reach out to customers. In the coming chapters, we will discuss in-depth how to make your mark in this industry. From segmenting the market and finding your niche, writing a business plan and finding shippers and carriers, we will cover everything you need to know. If you have never written a business plan before, we will also work on a template you can use to create your first.

So, is it really worth it, investing your time and money into freight brokerage? Yes, it is. Before you begin, however, you must take time and learn the basics of this industry. Like any other business, you cannot go in blindly and hope to succeed. This is a considerable investment on your part, and it is only fair that you give it the attention it deserves.

Chapter 3
The Importance of Knowing Your Target Market

In the earlier chapters, we mentioned the importance of connections and networks in the freight brokerage business. Adding to that, it is worth mentioning that this is an industry where your reputation is equally important. Reliability is one of the essential traits that will get you the kind of attention you need to grow your venture. Carriers need assurances that you will always pay their dues on time. Shippers, on the other hand, are more concerned about the safety of their cargo.

It might feel like this kind of reputation is only achievable after being in the industry for years, but that is not necessarily true. You can actually kickstart your career within the first year by understanding your market and shifting your focus to specific segments. With some research, you can identify sectors that are underserved by large firms in the market. You will also learn some of the challenges that the established firms have in meeting such groups' needs and capitalize on them. This is the principle of niche marketing.

Niche (Micro) Marketing

It is easier to grow your freight brokerage business by identifying a niche and focusing on meeting your customers' needs. Naturally, when you start this operation, it might seem like you are shifting your attention from the wider market, but that is not the case. Focusing on a select group makes it easier to understand and address their concerns better. It is also one of the most reliable ways of keeping a steady flow of business.

Benefits of Niche Marketing

The fact that you serve a given market segment daily gives you a better perspective of the players in that sector and their needs. With this understanding, you are better placed to address unique needs that large companies can't due to the diseconomies of scale. This experience and expertise go a long way in building customer trust, confidence and growing a reputation for your business and your brand. If you diligently keep at it, you will end up with a network of reliable carriers, shippers, and other strategic partners, like bankers, who help you grow your brokerage business.

Generally, niche marketing allows you to avoid wastage through special marketing efforts. Instead of scattering your marketing effort everywhere, you focus on an approach that will yield results. Broad marketing involves a lot of wastage because, most of the time, the majority of the recipients barely listen to you. Through niche marketing, you can use tools like emotional appeals to reach a specific audience.

- **High return on investment (ROI)**

By shifting your marketing efforts to a specific target group, you address their needs better, making them more likely to do business with you than conventional advertisers. In the beginning, it might seem counterproductive to have a smaller target audience, but with time, you realize that your conversion rate is better than a broad marketing approach. This is how to get and maintain a high ROI.

Apart from the customer approach, niche marketing is also easier on your budget. Compared to mass marketing, you spend less on niche marketing, even if you use the same marketing outlets. For example, TV ads cost more for a wider audience, when in the real sense, most of them will not pay attention to you.

- **Brand visibility**

Niche marketing helps you to improve your presence in the industry by enhancing your visibility. Generally, businesses that serve a niche market tend to offer unique services, making them stand out. In this way, you have an opportunity to present yourself before the right customers, which makes more business sense than presenting yourself in front of the mass market. The more people who are aware of your services, the higher the likelihood they will recommend you to their friends, families and associates, especially if their needs align with your offering.

- **Customer loyalty**

If there is one reason why you should consider niche marketing, it is customer loyalty. By design, niche marketing helps you to put the needs of your customers first. You listen to them and take care of their needs better than the more prominent companies can. Through niche marketing, you can address customer concerns at a personal level. Remember, we talked about this being an industry that's big on networking and connections. Customer loyalty plays a huge role in this. Besides, by offering unique services to your customers, you stand out from the competition.

- **Growth through word of mouth**

Niche marketing is big on word of mouth advertising. You will realize that people in a given niche are often in contact with one another. It is more or less similar to creating a close-knit community around your brokerage service. This gives you more opportunities to talk about your business and introduce new services to your clientele. For example, if the shippers or carriers express some concern to which you have a unique solution, they will soon become your best brand ambassadors. By serving them better and offering unique solutions, you can earn recommendations from their circles.

- **Less competition**

You will encounter less competition in niche mass marketing. From the onset, you start your brokerage firm on a growth trajectory. Mass marketing does work, but it is more effective for larger companies and brands that have been in the market longer. Bearing this in mind, you can consider mass marketing once you grow your brand.

- **Improved experiences**

In principle, niche marketing demands a concentrated approach in a given sector. This means that you will hone your expertise in a short time and become an expert in the field. Take note that most customers are enticed by your knowledge and experience in the field over the brand name. When you become an expert in a field, you will earn more than the customers' trust, and you also get brand recognition in the process.

Doing everything that everyone else is doing can only make you an average freight broker, at best. That's the risk of blending in with the crowd. However, if you are bold enough to focus on solving typical shipper and carrier problems better and faster than everyone else, you will stand out.

Possible Challenges in Niche Marketing

You should not take niche marketing as a blanket strategy for growing your business even with these benefits. As successful as niche marketing is for your business, there are some risks that you must be aware of. You need customers to grow, and by narrowing down your attention to a niche, you have a better chance of growing your brand faster. However, you are basically attending to a smaller market through niche marketing, which translates to slower or stunted growth. Given your demographic limits, it might take you longer to scale the heights you envisioned in your business plan.

- **Market vulnerability**

Venturing into niche marketing means taking more risks than the average freight broker. You peg all your hopes on succeeding with this niche approach. The challenge here is that you are putting all your eggs in one basket. While niche marketing can be a springboard to success, you are more vulnerable to drastic changes in the market, especially those that do not favor your target audience.

Another challenge with this vulnerability is that as much as it carries the prospect of a higher ROI, that return is not guaranteed. Because of the small market size, you might struggle to make large profit margins. It will be even harder to expand your market share.

Besides, the concept of niche marketing means fewer customers, which might be a risky prospect for a new business.

- **Innovation risk**

If you decide to go with niche marketing, you must find a way to innovate. In niche marketing, you go against the norm, especially when everyone else is using mass marketing. You will end up with a uniquely segmented market, and for lack of competition, it becomes difficult to know whether or not you need to improve your services. After all, there are not many competitors pushing your brand to do better.

- **The success conundrum**

The whole point of niche marketing is to succeed in your venture. However, success comes at a price. If your marketing approach proves successful, you can expect increased interest and competition from other brokers, and from there, it won't be long before your niche is saturated.

In retrospect, there are always advantages and disadvantages to every business model. However, you need customers to grow your business. You cannot do anything because of the disadvantages of niche marketing. Learning about them helps you to preempt their occurrence and act accordingly. For a beginner freight broker, the best way to make a name for yourself in such a highly competitive industry is niche marketing. Monitor the market, grow your influence and as your reputation grows, you can scale up your marketing approach accordingly.

How to Choose a Niche

With the knowledge you have on niche marketing, the next step is choosing your brokerage firm's right niche. There are many ways to go about this. Some people learn to identify niches while going through freight broker training. Others know their target market much earlier. If you do not fall into either of these categories, do not despair. The gist of niche selection has nothing to do with the industry but is a personal assessment.

- **Personal assessment**

Evaluate your level of preparedness before you begin. This is where your personality comes in. Think in terms of your talent, interest, skills, and personality. This is not just to help you select the niche, but it will also help you stay motivated when things are not going according to plan, which in business can happen to anyone.

Starting a business is one of the most difficult things you can do. Many people have all the necessary resources and opportunities but never have the guts to go ahead. You are in a good place because you have taken the first step, starting the business. So, how do you apply your personal assessment to discover your niche? List down your passions, knowledge, skills and expertise. There are many niches out there, and choosing one you are not knowledgeable about or passionate about is the first step towards failure. We need to avoid that.

Choose a niche you understand, not just because it is interesting. In business, things get tough from time to time and passion subsides. Ask yourself whether you see yourself working in that niche over the next five or seven years.

How does your skill level and past experience come into play? Think of what you learned before and how you can use it to gain an advantage in the niche. In some cases, you might need additional training to fit into the niche that you desire.

- **Market research**

Your work doesn't end when you realize that your personal traits align with the desired niche. It doesn't end when you select the niche, either. You have to research and determine whether there is a market for that particular niche. In freight brokerage, there are many niches you can consider. For example, you can segment the market in terms of special cargo, regional niches, types of trucks you use, or the type of material or products that are shipped through your brokerage firm.

Next, you want to understand the unique value proposition your firm is offering customers. What makes you different from other brokers? Why should shippers work with you instead of other brokers? What do you offer that others do not? This is where you understand your strengths and gain an in-depth understanding of the competitors' weaknesses. It also helps you to know where your business will be more effective.

Passion for your business and the selected niche will only get you so far. Be careful not to choose a niche with a tiny customer base. This is important because, ultimately, your business will only be and remain viable to customers when you address their needs. Let's say, for example, that you are a huge fan of motorbikes. You can research and find out how they are handled from one point to the next, and narrow down your business concept. Find out whether demand and supply in the market is sustainable over time.

Your advantage, in this case, comes from knowledge and experience. Since you know so much about motorbikes and you are an enthusiast, you can easily offer unique services to shippers and carriers than someone else who lacks your kind of knowledge might not be able to offer.

- **Geographical niches**

One method that has worked for many freight brokers in the past is to focus on regional niches. It is easier to find customers within your region. You can consider the state or even your city. Study the market and understand the core businesses in your region. If you are a manufacturing hub, you can specialize in handling those products. It gets even better if you enjoy some of the manufactured or assembled things in your region.

At the same time, try not to spread yourself thin. While enthusiasm is a good thing, only take up businesses that you can handle, or you will damage your reputation. Do not commit to loads that you cannot handle to fulfill the customers' satisfaction.

- **Types of trucks and cargo**

Another method of niche selection is to consider the type of trucks used. There is quite a variety you can work with, including tankers, flatbeds, dry vans and so on. Start with the kind of truck you can handle comfortably and make a name for yourself in the process. This way it is easier to find carriers and shippers with whom to partner.

In the same way you considered different types of trucks, consider the types of cargo. Every type of cargo requires a unique handling procedure. For example, the procedure for handling motorbike cargo is not the same as dairy, meat, or eggs. This gives you a lot of room for consideration. Delicate and perishable goods like dairy, meat and eggs need special handling.

If you start with these, you will have to look for special trucks that can transport the cargo without a hitch. You also have to look for carriers who are comfortable transporting that kind of cargo. In many cases, shippers tend to give special instructions for handling such delicate products, so you can use that as a stepping stone to making your mark in that niche.

When serving a particular niche, you become an expert over time. Before you know it, you become the go-to guy in your space for certain types of cargo. Once you've established a reputation for solid dependability, your reach becomes much more significant.

There's one danger in niche marketing, though—you can become so focused that your total revenue could end up coming from a few sources. Learn from the niche haulers of the trucking industry. Less than 25%–30% of their revenues come from a single source; they keep it diversified even within the niche. With the vagaries of the economy, putting your eggs in one basket can spell disaster when something terrible happens, a reality that even large freight broker companies are not immune to.

The following are some essential questions whose answers will lead you in the right direction during niche selection:

1. What products or companies are you interested in? Do you have a close connection to those brands?

2. What do you know about the logistics operation of the brands that interest you? Are their most pressing needs currently being met? If not, what can you do to fulfill their needs better than any other broker?

3. What are the best sources of information on the companies, brands, or products you want to serve? What can you do to become an expert in the field?

4. Who benefits most from your brokerage service?

5. Can you profile your ideal customer? What are their needs, strengths and weaknesses? How do you benefit their operation by being their niche broker?

From your answers to these questions, you can draft a plan to reach out to the customers you have profiled. Find out the key decision-makers for the companies and brands, and get in touch with them.

Ahead of your meeting, prepare a brief introduction for your brokerage firm, highlighting the value you bring to their operation and how having you as their go-to broker will benefit their overall business strategy. The introduction aims to show them how you will prop their success, helping them streamline their operation. If you can do that, you will have them on board.

Is it possible to have more than one niche?

The market is so wide, and there are many niches that you can tap into. So, the answer to the question above is yes! You can immerse yourself in more than one niche. It does not matter that you are new to the brokerage industry. Take note, however, that the concept of niche marketing is about perfection. Invest your time in one niche, perfect it, and use the lessons and skills learned to grow into another niche.

Working towards more than one niche is a growth-minded approach that means you will continuously be looking for opportunities to diversify your brokerage business. With time, your business will grow, and in the process, it will be easier for you to find niches that are a natural fit to your expertise.

Growing niches can only mean one thing; that you are doing great. Customers who grow with you in your journey will most likely send you referrals, helping your business to grow exponentially, too.

The thing about niche marketing in the freight brokerage industry is that there are times when you will need to think outside the box. One example of this is learning how to use keywords to your advantage. Keywords are not only for online businesses. When marketing your freight brokerage business, you use all the tools available at your disposal. An essential tool in your arsenal is keyword research.

Keyword research helps you to determine how often people search for specific phrases online. You can also identify seasonal trends of those and related searches and use that information to identify the right niche in the process. You will look at impressions, clicks, and the value attached to them. This sounds like search engine optimization, but it is useful. If a few people are searching for particular keywords, they are probably low-value keywords. The lesson here is that there is not much in that niche to warrant your attention. It could be too niche, and you would price yourself out of the market.

As we advance, always know that your niche's ideal definition should correspond with you and your business' needs. You can use standard industry benchmarks for general insight and leave it at that because your competitors are probably not doing the same thing.

In terms of marketing your freight brokerage firm, there isn't much to choose between niche marketing and mass marketing. It all comes down to what is right at that moment. They are both effective, depending on how you use them. What's mandatory on your part is proper planning, research, and with the right tools, you can use niche marketing to grow your brokerage firm and become the brand everyone wants to work with.

Chapter 4
Let's Talk About Money

The freight brokerage industry is the backbone of many businesses in the country. Before going into this business, you should be aware of the costs involved to plan your finances accordingly. One of the first things you should think about is the location of your business. Today, many people work from home, in light of the recent pandemic. If you find this appropriate, it will save you on office setup costs. That being said, you might want to lease an office, in which case there will be other costs to look at. If you are hiring a team of employees, you will also have to plan for salaries and other related expenses.

Start-up Costs

So, the biggest question on your mind is how much you should set aside to start your freight brokerage business. The total sum varies from one individual to the next, depending on your preferences. To make your work easier, let's look at the components of your expenditure list and, at the end of this chapter, we will determine the total cost of setting up.

Business Registration

You must first register the business with the Secretary of State, from where you will receive a tax number and registration from the department of revenue in your state. Assuming you will also operate as a carrier, you must get a permit from the DMV. The total registration costs vary from one state to the next and cost up to $300. Other costs, including that of registering a tax number, are set differently by each state.

Brokerage License

Upon application, the Federal Motor Carrier Safety Administration (FMCSA) grants you the license to operate as a freight broker. This is to certify your qualifications and authorizes you to operate as a freight broker or carrier.

You can apply for this license in two categories: a property broker or household goods broker. While you can apply for whichever suits your needs, it makes sense to apply for both and a carrier license if you have your own trucks. The license fee is $300 for each of the authorities.

On top of that, you also need to set aside $60–$80 for the annual Unified Carrier Registration (UCR), which applies to freight carriers and brokers.

Annual Surety Bond

To protect all the stakeholders' interests in the industry, the FMCSA set a surety bond of $75,000, which is an agreement between the freight broker, surety company, and authorities. The surety bond is safeguarded against any form of misconduct that any of the parties might suffer if the freight broker breaches set industry rules and regulations. Note, however, that both your business and yourself are not protected under this surety. It is basically to protect your customers and the licensing authority.

$75,000 sounds steep for someone who is just setting up a business, right? Well, you only have to pay a fraction of it. The amount you pay will depend on your credit rating, industry experience, and financial history on other credit facilities you might have. People with a good credit score can pay up to 4% ($3000), and as low as 1% ($750) annually. With bad credit, you can pay up to 12% ($9000) annually. If you start at 12%, you can reduce your annual premiums by working on improving your credit.

Cargo and Liability Insurance (Optional)

It is good practice to get insurance when going into a business. According to the FMCSA, however, getting cargo, liability, or property insurance is not mandatory. So, what should you do? Think in terms of insurance value. There's that peace of mind, knowing that you are protected in the event of freight damage or an irresponsible carrier. While this insurance cover is optional, having it gives your shippers confidence that yours is a legitimate business—this can earn you more business.

On average, insurance policies for cargo will cost around $1500 a year. You might also spend a similar amount on property and liability policies. Note, however, that if you hire employees, it is mandatory to have workers' compensation insurance.

While a surety bond protects the authorities and your customers, you are protected by the business insurance cover you take. Other than workers' compensation, other forms of business insurance you can take include property insurance and general liability coverage. If you are working from home, talk to your insurer about a relevant home-based insurance cover.

Office and Office Equipment

The cost of setting up an office depends on the kind of equipment you need. On average, you can set up a small office for around $1000. Next, you will look at monthly recurring expenditures, including assorted equipment, stationery, and utility bills. For this, you can expect to spend around $500.

Office expenses largely depend on the type of setup you are working with. Thinking of office space, working from home will significantly reduce your expenditure. Most brokers today use their personal phones to keep in touch with business partners. With a laptop and a small desk at home, you might cut out a massive chunk from your office and equipment budget.

Speaking of your laptop or computer, you don't need something fancy. A device with 8GB of RAM and a core i5 processor should be more than sufficient. Building on that, you need proper storage. Today, there are lots of cloud storage options you can use, both premium and freemium services. This will help you with regular backups, so your data is always safe.

Licensed Brokerage Software

While they are not mandatory, look into brokerage software. We live in a world where you cannot ignore the disruptive impact and importance of technology in your industry. Software solutions exist to make your work easier. The complete package should include a transportation management system (TMS) and a customer relationship manager (CRM). You will also need a load board to connect you with available and qualified carriers for cargo. So far, most players in the industry swear by DAT and TruckStop. You can sign up for a load board for around $50.

These software solutions offer greater efficiency in managing your business. You can start with simple software solutions and scale up as your business grows. On average, you should spend between $1000 and $3000 on software annually.

Training

While freight brokerage training is optional, it will be useful if you have never worked in the industry in any capacity before, either as a motor carrier or a broker. Some of the skills you will learn include compliance with legal guidelines in your jurisdiction and how to manage the brokerage firm. The training cost varies from one institution to the other, the course content and material, and range from $200 to $1500, or higher.

Marketing

Marketing is key to the growth of your freight brokerage business. Considering the importance of establishing strong networks, you must find a way to promote your business. Referrals and word of mouth will work, and for the most part, they are effective. However, these are highly effective if you have an established network of customers and other transportation industry professionals.

For a new business, you will have to pay for marketing services. Towards this end, plan for a website, attend networking events and try to join load boards. You can also use your social media outlets. You can get a simple website from $300 onwards. While in the design stage, ensure your developer builds a website that loads fast and offers users all the information they need at a glance.

Accounting Tools

You will need to account for the way money moves in and out of your business. This is where accounting tools are useful. One option is to hire an accountant to help you either on a full-time basis or on a contract basis. However, if you do not have that much money to spare, many accounting tools are simple, easy to use and affordable. One of these is QuickBooks.

QuickBooks is so easy to use, you don't need accounting experience to make the most use of it. You can also find tutorial videos online and on YouTube that will give you the best introduction to the accounting suite. Accounting tools are essential in your business because they help you to prepare clean financial records. On average, you might spend around $50 a month on this, depending on the suite you use.

From our discussion above, we can now summarize the estimated costs of setting up your operation as follows:

- Rent: $0–$1,000
- Equipment: $6,000–$22,000
- Licenses/tax deposits: $200–$400
- Advertising/marketing: $500–$1,500
- Utilities/phone: $100–$300
- Professional services: $200–$750
- Payroll: $0–$5,000
- Supplies: $300–$500
- Insurance (first quarter): $700–$1,400
- Suggested operating capital: $5,000–$250,000 (cash or line of credit)

Remember that these costs are just estimates, meant to guide you. The actual figures will depend on different features, especially your location and personal preferences for your operation.

The Profit

Going into any business, one of the most important things to consider is profit. It is not just about how much you will make from the business but, more importantly, about sustainability. Note that unless you explicitly register your business as such, you are neither a shipper nor a carrier but a middleman who ensures the aforementioned parties have their needs met. Since your work ensures carriers earn more money by keeping their trucks full and shippers get access to reliable carriers, the next step is to look into the profit margins. Let's make one thing clear: Unless you are employed under someone, you do not earn a salary in this industry. Brokers earn commissions.

According to the U.S Bureau of Labor Statistics projections, the future is bright for freight brokers. The industry has been on an upward growth trajectory. This means there is more room for you to make money.

How much do I take home?

One of the top questions on your mind is probably how much you will earn in this business. Given that freight brokers earn commissions, it is virtually impractical to calculate an accurate annual income. That notwithstanding, PayScale, Indeed and Glassdoor estimate that freight brokers bring in anywhere between $30,000 and $92000 a year. Many factors determine how much you earn in this industry, so it is possible to earn much more or even less. For example, brokers in the bigger cities, like Portland and Kansas City, earn more than their counterparts in the smaller cities. This is due to things like the volume and frequency of business you can conduct in a given time.

That being said, the national average annual earnings for freight brokers is around $62,105. On commission, you can rake in an extra $28,000 every year.

This is an industry where your earnings are directly proportional to your input and effort into the business. Many freight brokers earn six-figure salaries, yet they work from home. This caliber of brokers has a good reputation and have been in the business longer. You can join that league by taking your work seriously. You can grow your business and have agents working for you for commissions of up to 15%.

The figures above notwithstanding, your average income comes down to factors like your experience level, your customers' profitability, your gross revenue, business structure and reputation in the market. To understand this better, let's look at your position in terms of the three types of brokers in the industry below. The assumption here is that each of the brokers conducts the same amount of business. For the purpose of this discussion, we will assume an annual revenue of $2,000,000, and with a 17.5% margin, an annual gross profit of $350,000.

1. **The W-2 Broker**

You will realize that there are more W-2 brokers in the market than all the other categories, with most large freight brokerage companies operating in this category. Practically, this is a company that hires personnel in different sales and operations capacities. They also own the customer accounts and run all the business operations but offer the brokers office space.

As a W-2 broker, you might earn a basic salary and a commission based on your company's profits. On average, W-2 brokers earn around $40,000, with an extra 13% in commission of the gross profits.

From our sales and gross profit projections earlier, at 13%, your annual income translates to:

$40,000 + $45,500 = $85,500

Why should you consider getting into the business as a W-2 broker? Well, since you will be an employee, you are on a payroll and like every other employee, you earn a basic salary. The base salary gives you a guarantee, especially if you are new to the industry and are uncertain about your productivity. The commissions are a bonus based on your effort and input into the business. Another benefit is that most companies will pay for your training courses.

That being said, your employer retains most of the profit, and you might also have to sign a non-compete clause in your contract to protect your employer's interests and to prevent you from moving to a competitor with their customers.

2. **The Licensed Broker**

A licensed broker is a business owner, meaning that you will assume all the risks associated with the business. With all the necessary assets, you can scale the business accordingly over the years. Operating as a licensed owner means there is as great a chance of success as there is of failure. There are no independent contractors or employees.

In this case, you must be licensed by the Department of Transportation. As discussed earlier, you will also obtain a surety bond and apply for all other services necessary to run the business, including insurance. We discussed most of the costs that you will incur earlier in this chapter. The challenge comes in realizing how much you have to invest in the business without earning anything yet.

For licensed brokers, costs typically pile up so fast, so you might have to look into additional means of financing the operation. Most successful licensed brokers have loyal customers. It is your responsibility to run all the business functions, or hire staff to assist, where necessary. This model's beauty is that you enjoy 100% of what remains after accounting for expenses and other relevant deductions. You also shoulder 100% of the burden if you are making losses.

Many licensed brokers fold up in less than three years because they don't have sufficient recurring revenue to keep the business running or insufficient start-up cash. Here's what your financial year might look like:

Total operating expenses

DoT Authorities	$300
Bond	$10,000
Insurance	$3,000
Software	$7,500
Load boards	$3,600
Factoring	$70,000
Wages	$40,000
Total	**$134,400**

Profit & Loss Assessment

Revenue	$2,000,000
Carriers	($1,650,000)
Gross profit	**$350000**
Expenses	($134,400)

Net Earnings	**$215,600**

In this example, you take home $215,600 annually.

3. **The 1099 Agent**

In this category, you work as an independent contractor, but for a licensed broker. This category has grown relatively popular in recent years. The licensed broker assumes all the costs discussed above, but the broker business is handled either by an agent, or a group of agents.

Most of your work involves finding freight and moving it through carriers, so you can pretty much work from home. The licensed agent handles all the back-office tasks like marketing, claims handling, billing, tech support, collections, etc. Your role as an agent is restricted to sales and operations, which you can also sub-contract if you need to.

While this model offers more flexibility than the other two, it is not your best bet as a beginner. You must bring in your customers and organize their schedules, including the dispatch trucks. Earnings in this category are commission-based, with some of the top agents earning up to 70%, with the licensed broker retaining the rest to cover business expenses. On average, 1099 agents can take home more than $200,000 a year.

Having looked at all the categories, which one works for you? More importantly, you can now understand the difference in earning structures for freight brokers. As exciting as these figures are, you must also note that they were hypothetical. It might take you a while to earn $2 million, probably not in your first year of operation. Since you do not have to deal with office logistics, many brokers today operate as 1099 agents, using the resources saved to focus on growing their customer database.

The Pricing

Having discussed the costs and possible profit margins, you need to take a closer look at the money. One of the most important relationships that will help you to succeed is with your banker. You need a good relationship with your banker to succeed in the freight brokerage business. You will need a line of credit to pay carriers before you receive anything from the shippers from time to time. With a good relationship, you can count on your banker for a quick $300,000 in such times. Note that without securing carriers' payment on time, they will avoid your freight. Without carriers, you have no business. Therefore, as much as you will be looking at insurance, licenses and other costs, you should prioritize finding a good banker who understands your business's nature and can assist on short notice.

How do you handle this? First, a bank you have never done business with will be apprehensive. Even your usual bank will be apprehensive if you do not have a business plan. Another factor that will make things easier for you is your credit record. This is important because the freight brokers typically do not have any assets the bank can repossess if you default on payments. Your business plan should include a profile package that shows the bank you are creditworthy and, by opening a line of credit for you, they will also get good business in return.

That being said, how do you determine freight charges? These are generally based on the load weight and the distance the carriers will move it. Other factors that determine freight charges include the type of truck requested for that particular cargo and the number of stops the driver must make to pick up and deliver the load.

Shipments are generally moved on a one pickup one delivery basis without incurring additional charges. If the carrier must make extra stops, you can discuss and negotiate the terms and charges with them. It is wise to study the market and know the prevailing shipping rates and specifications for the kind of cargo you will haul. Contact a few carriers and compare their rates and tariffs for this.

Since you are paid on commission, you can either bill the shipper the carrier's cost plus your commission or have the carrier bill the shipper and then pay your commission. Since the latter is cumbersome, most freight brokers bill customers after the carrier bills them. Note that while commissions are negotiable, they are not the net earnings. Commissions earned are part of your gross earnings. From there, you must account for overheads like rent, debts, utility bills, sales commissions, payroll processing, taxes and so on.

Chapter 5
Writing a Business Plan

A business plan is an important step towards the success of your brokerage firm. This is a plan that gives an in-depth description of your business. Investors and financiers generally look at your business plan to determine whether your business is sound enough to warrant their support. We mentioned earlier in the book that you need to have a good relationship with your banker in this industry. From time to time, you will need a line of credit to keep things running. Without a business plan, your bank cannot ascertain the viability of your business. While you need a business plan when starting your brokerage firm, you can also revise it and write a new one once your operation is running.

For a start-up like yours, a business plan is a necessary document because it gives you direction. An elaborate business plan should tell someone how you plan to handle the financial, marketing and operational tasks. Other than that, it should give an accurate description of the business, the services that you offer, and how you intend to achieve your objectives.

When writing the plan, make sure you include a section on the industry overview. Investors have their own assessment of the industry and would like to compare your assessment with theirs. Usually, if you are both on the same page, it is easier to convince them to come on board. Besides the comparative concept of the industry analysis, you also must highlight the nature of competition in the segment you are investing in and how you plan to differentiate yourself while adding value to the end-users.

It is quite unfortunate that many small business owners ignore the business plan when setting up their venture. This is an important document that influences your brokerage business's beginning, growth, and sustained development over the years, so take your time and create a good one.

Value and Importance of Having a Business Plan

Financing your operation through loans or luring investors is not the only reason you should have a business plan. As a business owner, this simple document offers more value to you than you might realize. All the stakeholders in your venture have something to gain from the business plan.

Take note that your business plan does not necessarily have to be elaborate. It should be a simple document that captures the true state and nature of your business. On the same note, it should be simple enough that you can review it from time to time and update it as your operation grows. Below, we will highlight some of the benefits of having a business plan, and in the process, you will realize how valuable this document is:

1. **Business overview**

A good business plan should give you a complete overview of your operation. Each aspect of your business is interconnected. For example, from your strategic plan, someone should be able to see how your marketing plan is connected to achieving your business goals. The same applies to your sales. There should be a direct relationship between your marketing expenditure and sales. Essentially, a glimpse at the business plan should give you a bigger picture of the business.

Other than an overview of your business, the plan should also help you to identify and maintain your identity throughout the operation. Business identity is about your target market, the unique brokerage services that you offer and so on. This guides you along the way if you ever need a reality check on the nature of your business.

2. **Clear priorities**

Running your brokerage firm as a sole proprietor, everything rests on your shoulder. It is easy to get swamped in all that's going on around you. However, the business plan is a reminder that you cannot do everything at the same time. You can run the business and handle everything on your own, but you must have clear priorities to succeed. Through the business plan, you keep track of all the important procedures and activities. In essence, it helps you manage your effort, time, and other resources accordingly.

3. **Change management**

A proper business plan is necessary to help you make the required adjustments to your business from time to time. It keeps you in check. New developments, progress tracking, and frequent reviews are necessary to help you adjust your business process according to your customer's needs and the industry demands. More often, you will go back to your actual vs. plan analysis and make changes relevant to the prevailing conditions. Your business plan reminds you of your business's overall objectives, such that even with the changes made, you still stay on course towards realizing the business goals.

4. **Accountability**

The business plan holds you accountable for all your actions. It spells out the expectations of running the brokerage firm. A successful business is a result-oriented business. You will use the business plan for regular reviews to ensure that you are still on course. Note that challenges and disappointments are normal in business, and it is in such moments that you can look to your business plan and review progress so far. When the outlook seems fuzzy, the plan is a reminder of where you need to be.

5. Money management

For someone running their first business, it is easy to get caught up in the allure of cash flows. Seeing the profits streaming in is a good feeling. However, business is about more than that. You must account for purchases, honor your debt obligations, ensure carriers are paid on time, and take care of petty cash purchases, among other things.

Your business's monetary position should be such that it can run on its own without requiring additional financial injection from elsewhere. If you realize that you constantly have to seek financing, yet you are operating normally, something might be amiss. For example, some customers pay after services are rendered. How many such customers do you have?

Slow-paying customers keep your money on hold, forcing you to operate on debt, which is not a good position for your business. The business plan helps you to identify such challenges and make adjustments. You can talk to such customers about adjusting their payment terms, probably introducing reminders and penalties for late payments. Everyone is in the business of making money. Do not allow customers to exert unnecessary strain on your finances. You might keep them happy and keep them over the long term, but in the process, you miss the opportunity to grow your business because your funds are tied up in their operations.

6. **Milestones**

Break down your targets into achievable milestones. Milestones are the small wins you achieve on your way to greater wins. You cannot succeed overnight. Long-term business success is achieved by small milestone wins that compound into the overall success.

Let's say your overall plan is to grow your freight brokerage firm in three years. Some of the milestones you can work around include securing contracts with some big shippers or carriers, raising a given amount of cash from business operations, or growing your presence in the region. Each time you achieve one of these milestones, you are one step closer to realizing your long-term goals. Besides, milestones give you small but visible, tangible goals that you can achieve.

7. **Metrics**

Your business plan should also include performance indicators you can frequently review to determine whether you are heading in the right direction. Performance indicators are generally in numbers, so you need to identify the critical numbers for your business. For example, the number of customers, size of debt and repayment are some of the easy picks. Going further, other metrics you can monitor include conversion rates and traffic online, the number of complaints received and so on. The business plan outlines steps you will take towards success. The metrics are proof that you are doing well or not. These are useful evaluators for any business.

Starting the brokerage firm might have been one of the biggest challenges you have taken so far, but that's not the end of it. Keeping the firm alive and steering it to growth and success is even more challenging. Ultimately, a business plan helps you to maintain a strategic focus on your objectives, and in the process, offer customers quality brokerage services.

Types of Business Plans

We have looked at the value you derive from a business plan as an essential tool in your pursuit of growth and success in the freight industry. From management guides to attracting investors, this is an important document you must prepare with a lot of care. Depending on your needs and the operation, there are different types of business plans you can create. We will look at the major categories below.

1. **Start-Up Business Plans**

When starting a new business, you must outline how you get from idea to concept and implementation. This is where a start-up business plan comes in handy. This type of business plan will describe your business, the kind of brokerage services you offer, the management process and an honest review of the market.

Your start-up plan is incomplete without a financial analysis. Do not just dream up numbers, do some research and find out how other brokerage firms manage their operations. Include a financial analysis that outlines your cash flow projections, expected income, sales and profit.

2. **Internal Business Plans**

These plans are written for an internal audience in the business. For example, you can have a business plan for the marketing department to help plan your upcoming or continued marketing efforts. Internal business plans talk about the present state of the business, profitability, operating costs, etc. From this plan, you come up with strategies on how to raise or repay the capital. Ideally, this plan is pegged on the general market size, the level of influence you have on the market, and how this affects your income.

Under this category, we also have an operational business plan. This is another internal plan that addresses the factors critical to your operation. More importantly, this plan highlights your targets, deadlines and markers for the business calendar year. This is also the plan that discusses the roles and responsibilities of all members of your firm.

3. **Strategic Business Plans**

Strategic plans are geared towards the overall growth of the business. They highlight your goals for the freight brokerage business and how you can achieve them. Strategy formulation is key to business success because it lays the foundation for everything you will do. The outline and format of a strategic business plan vary from one business to the next, but they must all discuss the following:

- Your vision
- Mission statement
- Key success factors
- How to meet your objectives
- Implementation schedule

The main objective of strategy formulation is to shed light on each level or department's roles in your business and their contribution towards your ultimate goals. It can also present that rallying call for your team members to pull their weight and work towards the business goals.

4. **Feasibility Business Plans**

Feasibility reports the possibility of success in your brokerage venture. This is done by determining the market for your brokerage services and whether you can profit from the venture. This plan analyzes the need for your services in the market, your target audience, and the capital needed to meet those objectives. This plan is not limited to these metrics. Anything that helps you gauge the market readiness for your business's services and profitability can make it to the feasibility business plan. The metrics culminate into recommendations on how to penetrate the market and make a profit.

5. **Growth Business Plans**

As the name suggests, this plan takes a futuristic approach to the business. It is about growth projections, and for varying reasons, you prepare it for both internal and external use. Let's say you seek capital injection into the business. Your growth plan must show prospective investors a complete description of your company, the staff and management. Investors need to understand your growth plan.

You start by highlighting the targets you set for your business and show how the current business setup will help you realize that plan. You can also include revenue and expense estimates. From your projections, a growth-minded business should have enough money to stay afloat after paying all business expenses and any other financial obligations.

Lean Business Plan

As the name suggests, a lean business plan includes only the essential things your business needs. This is a watered-down version of the general business plan we have discussed in this chapter. The lean business plan is geared towards addressing the core functions of the business. Therefore, it is scanty on descriptions and is often presented to lenders and investors to give them a quick glance at the business and its position. Lean business plans are prepared for management optimization.

The lean business plan is essentially the only business plan you will ever need. Do not hurry to create a formal and lengthy business plan. It is advisable to start lean, and as the business grows, you can update the plan to reflect the new position. Below are the features of a lean business plan:

1. Strategy

A small business is easier to manage than a large business. This is because you have a bird's eye view of everything that goes on. Keep this in mind when writing the business. The smaller the business, the easier it is to avoid distractions. When writing this plan, strategy formulation is as simple as noting down bullet points. They act as quick reminders of what needs to be done and how to go about it.

The thing about strategy formulation is that it will guide all your effort going forward. Do not make the mistake of working outside the strategy plan. You will waste resources you might never recover. For strategy formulation, first figure out your business identity. This stays with you for as long as the business is in operation. Next, think about your customers and, finally, the product or service you are offering.

2. Tactics

Building on strategy formulation, work on the tactics. The strategy will still influence the approaches you use to achieve your goals. You know what your business is about and what you cannot do. You also know the target audience, so from here, come up with an action plan on how to bring the strategies to life. It is at this stage that you think about executing the business plan.

There are many tactics you can think about. Let's take marketing, for example. Consider things like the positioning of your message, service pricing, target market, how to differentiate your business from everyone else in an industry that is saturated with brokers. How will you handle sales? How do you blend traditional and effective marketing approaches with modern marketing tactics to get the best returns?

Next, you think about the product or service you are offering. How do you introduce it into the market? Are you planning a launch? Is the launch date good enough? Do you need a website, vendors, or a different delivery option when launching the business?

Everything in your business depends on the money. How are your financial plans? Do you have a good working relationship with your bank? Can they extend you a line of credit to take care of your obligations?

Note that the responses to these questions will be guided by strategy formulation. By now, you can see how interconnected every aspect of a lean business plan is. This means that you should think through all the factors involved before committing to anything. The purpose of a lean business is to limit wastage.

3. Assumptions, Milestones, Metrics, and Schedule

Once you write down the tactics, go over them again. In this section, you will add specifics to the tactics so that your effort can come to fruition. An effective plan for your tactics should have deadlines and other specifics that make them tangible.

First, work on a review schedule. This is important because things hardly go according to plan. You can remember the number of times you have had to go back on some plan because something changed. The same applies in business, especially where money is involved. You must schedule a review at regular intervals to keep up with the progress and growth in the business. If you foresee something will not happen as planned, reorganize it as appropriate.

You will make some assumptions when creating a lean business plan. Note them down on a list so that they are easier to review whenever you need to. Once the plan is in motion, track and review the results, and if they are not similar to your plan, which is most often the case, go back to the list of assumptions and identify what might have changed.

When working with assumptions, you hope that things will go according to plan, but this is not always the case. Once you identify the changes, revise the plan and monitor progress thereon for future review. Even as you look at the assumptions, you must also check to ensure that your plan was properly executed.

Milestones are about accountability. What activities must be completed by a certain time, and more importantly, who is responsible for them? Milestones help keep you in check and break down big tasks into smaller chunks that are easier to handle. They act as reminders, commitments that will get you closer to realizing your goal. Some of the milestones you can have in this case include the start and end dates, when to review budgets, and so on. This is the first point at which your management skills are called into accountability.

Finally, you have to look at the key metrics in your business. These are the performance yardsticks that inform you whether you are doing well or not. Metrics also help in management accountability. At this point, you will be looking at things like expenses, costs, and sales. If you have a website for your brokerage firm, the metrics you can consider include website traffic, referrals, conversion rates, tweets, impressions, and likes. There is an endless list of things you can consider, so try to tailor the factors to suit your brokerage business.

4. Forecasts of Sales, Costs, Expenses, and Cash

To keep the business running, you must be able to monitor and manage the money. Planning for the money helps you to make projections for the future based on current events. Without forecasting, it is impossible to track pertinent problems, results or capitalize on situations that put you at an advantage in the market.

You don't have to overthink the forecast. Since you are starting a small business, a simple forecast of costs and sales is good enough. It does not have to be accurate either, but it should be realistic so that you work within an acceptable business range.

With forecasting, you will be wrong most of the time when you look at the actual results, and this is okay. The lesson here is to review the results and identify how far your assumptions were from the real outcome. With time and experience, you will realize that your assumptions and real results are relatively close, which is a sign that you have a good grasp of the business's key factors.

With forecasting, you also have to make projections for cash flow. You cannot run the business without the money. The emphasis here is mostly about running a profitable business. Simply put, try to keep your expenses lower than your costs. The challenge most businesses face, and which you will come to realize soon enough in the freight brokerage industry, is that you usually don't get paid on the exact date you expected. At the same time, you cannot wait until you have money before you can make purchases. Therefore, the fact that you have money in the bank is not a guarantee that your business is making profits.

Freight Broker Business Plan Template

The outline below is a simple template that you can use to create a freight brokerage firm's business plan. Having looked at a lean business plan before, note that you do not have to include everything in this plan from the onset. However, as the business grows, you can update your plan with respect to the growth trajectory.

A. Executive Summary

Skip this section and write it once you complete the entire plan. It should be an overview of your business, addressing the what, why and how you will succeed. It is the highlight of your company and a crucial section if you pitch the business idea to investors.

B. Business Description and Vision

This section captures the intricate details of your freight business. When someone goes through your business plan, they should understand your core values. This is also where you introduce the growth potential of your business.

1. Mission Statement
2. Company Vision

3. Business Goals and Objectives
4. Brief Background History

C. Definition of the Market

To define your market, think about the niche you want to serve, how to reach your customers, and your projections in terms of expanding your reach. Fill this section by addressing the following aspects:

1. Industry and industry prospects
2. Potential market share
3. Target market segments
4. Target customers
5. Customer challenges and needs you are addressing
6. Key competitor profiles

D. Description of Services

The freight business is a service-centered business, which gives you a lot of room to differentiate your services from other brokers in the market. This section gives the investor confidence because they understand what your business is about, why you are in it, your competitive edge, and its value proposition. Under this section, you will discuss the following:

1. Description of Services
2. Pricing Strategy

3. Competitive Advantage

E. Strategic Direction

This section is about the SWOT analysis for your brokerage business. Analyze your business in the context of the market and industry in general. You can also propose services you plan to introduce in the future. You will discuss the following:

1. Strengths of the Freight Brokerage Firm
2. Weaknesses
3. Opportunities in the Marketplace
4. Threats
5. Future Growth Prospects

F. Marketing and Sales Strategy

In this section, you describe how you intend to grow and market the business. You will talk about the different marketing forms you plan to use, sales and advertising strategies, public relations, and promotions where applicable. You will also mention who your market is, and how to reach customers. Ensure you highlight how to make your business competitive, given the nature of competition in the industry. In this section, you will discuss the following:

1. Market Description
2. Service Demand

3. Marketing Strategy
4. Promotions Strategy
5. Sales Strategy
6. Internet Marketing Strategy
7. Strategic Alliances

G. Organization and Management

How you organize your business will determine your profitability in the market over the years. Organization management includes things like proper record keeping, accounting and billing tasks. This section informs investors of how you will run the business on a day to day basis. The outline of your business should also consider the legal status of your business. You will discuss the following in this sector:

1. Business Structure
2. Management Team and Roles
3. Organizational Structure
4. Personnel Plan, including freight agents
5. Legal Process Agents and States of Operation
6. Corporate Legal Representative

H. Financial Management

Under financial management, you should explain the numbers to your investors. This is the trickiest part of the business plan because the numbers must add up.

Consider the fact that investors generally have a capable team of analysts who will vet your business plan to determine whether you are a suitable candidate for their investment.

This section should show them the expected returns so that they can make plans on how to recoup their investment. They also need to see your business's financial viability and, more importantly, your bottom line projections. Since you are just starting the business, it makes sense to work with estimates and highlight them as such. You generally have no idea what the business will look like in the foreseeable future, so it is only fair that you work with estimates. Based on your business estimates, you can prepare an income statement, balance sheet and cash flow statement.

In case you have been in the business for some time and you are probably looking for an investor to support your growth objectives, you should prepare financial reports for the past three years. If you are talking to your banker, the loan managers would be interested in looking at your personal financial statements. This gives them a better picture of the person behind the business. It is more or less their way of conducting a lifestyle audit on you. It helps them determine whether you can run a successful business or use proceeds from the business to furnish a lavish lifestyle, rendering you an unworthy candidate for their financial support.

Going through the business plan, you realize how crucial it is to think rationally and discipline yourself when managing the business. The hard work does not end at writing the business plan, either. For your business to succeed, you must follow through and review input and results from time to time.

Chapter 6
How to Find Carriers and Shippers

The next step in your business growth plan is to find regular shippers and carriers. This is the point where your business strategies come into effect. A steady flow of customers is every freight broker's dream, and to achieve that, you need to network and establish quality connections and relationships. Such relationships are built on trust and reliability, so even if you bring in a customer for the first transaction, treat them well to keep them around for the long haul.

While good marketing strategies will work for you, bad marketing is just as effective in chasing customers away. Therefore, before you get started on the strategy we will discuss in this section, you must make sure you have your marketing and communications strategies on point. For example, many first-time customers will check out your website. This is where you hit or miss. Keep things professional. You are a brand now, so try to operate your business as such.

Think of your perception when you interact with a company for the first time. The red flags you look for are the same things your customers are looking for to protect their investment. Have a professional website, logo and anything else that gives customers the best first impression of your brand. Ensure your social media pages align with the context on your website.

At any given point in time, many moving pieces in the logistics industry align to ensure that shippers, carriers and brokers move cargo from one point to another. Shippers rely on your expertise and experience in logistics, while on the other hand, you can choose those who meet the shippers' needs from your database of carriers.

You are the oil that keeps the wheels turning in this industry, and you must always act fast. So, how do you find the right carrier to move cargo for your customers? Let's look at some of the most reliable methods brokers have used over the years:

1. **Referrals and recommendations**

In this industry, your best customers are your best brand ambassadors. You are likely to get more leads from their business associates, friends and family members. When customers enjoy your services, they spread the word. Do not be afraid to ask them for referrals. Apart from that, establish a warm connection with them beyond the business. That way, you can use their name in your pitch to new customers for relevance and credibility. Apart from that, if your new prospects call your main customer, they will receive nothing but good words about your work. You can also reward customers for referrals.

2. **Warm calling**

People don't like cold calling, as much as it has worked for many businesses in the past. Imagine a company calling you out of the blue, pitching their business to you. Cold calls are often frowned upon because they are an inconvenience to the recipient, among other reasons. Instead of cold calling, why don't you try warm calling?

Look for a database of distributors and manufacturers in your region. Ensure the database is comprehensive, with more information about the target audience like relevant contact names and addresses, products they handle, revenues and so on. This database contains useful information about your potential customers and their immediate needs. Armed with this information, you can make that cold call, but since you know so much about them, appeal to their business needs. Offer them reliable and credible solutions. That is how you turn cold calls into successful warm calls.

3. **Use reference sheets**

Reference sheets contain names of company references when they sign credit applications. This is an excellent place to find shippers and carriers. From such lists, you can tell a company's profile and reputation by the number of times they are listed as references.

At the same time, you can also look towards other freight businesses in the market as your customers.

There's a good chance your customers are also looking for business, so learn from them and you might find new customers by looking at similar entities in the market. Besides, since you have experience in moving freight, they might want to talk to you and discuss options.

4. **Monitor the competition**

Before they become your customers, they probably take their business to another broker, so they might not need your services. However, this should not put you down. Everyone is always looking to cut costs, so recommend a free audit, without any obligation on their part. If you can beat their current freight broker's rates, they can either switch to your business or keep you on their list as a backup.

Remind the customer that you are on standby if anything ever goes wrong with their current broker. From your audit, it's also possible that you might not be at their current broker's rates and still remain profitable. That's okay because at least you will know what other brokers are charging and revise your rates accordingly.

5. **Check dormant accounts**

If you keep a list of customers you work with, identify those who used to work with you but have since gone silent. Reach out to them and find out why they moved on from you. If you had some issues, show them that you fixed them, and ask to bring them on again.

Accounts might also become dormant because the customers' primary contact had left the company, or a new company acquired the business. The customers might not be comfortable working with you because they don't know you. In this case, reach out to the former account handler and ask them to introduce the customers.

6. **Send direct mail**

One of the easiest ways of reaching out to a large target audience is through direct mail. Create a profile for shippers and carriers and purchase a list that would fit those profiles. Select those companies or individuals you wish to work with and send them an introduction letter or a postcard. This is also an excellent time to send a promotional offer.

The challenge with direct mail is that the results are not instant. You must be patient and even consider mailing the target audience once a month. Each time you send the mail, be creative and send a new letter. Apart from the mail, you should also call the potential customer for a formal introduction.

Two things might happen when you make that call. One, the customer might be interested and request further clarification. Second, they might not be interested. In the second option, ask the customer if they don't mind you checking in with them from time to time, hoping that they might change their mind. Alternatively, you can also ask them to suggest an appropriate time to reach out in the future.

The concept of direct mailing is to make the customer think of you if they ever need freight brokerage services. This is why you see companies sending cards and other kinds of mail during holidays, wishing customers prosperity and happiness.

7. **Build lasting relationships**

The transport industry is purely a relationship business. To succeed as a broker, you need to create solid relationships, not just with carriers but also with shippers and consignees. Remember that the aim is not only to get carriers to move cargo for you; you need to understand their business. You need to understand their values, too. Go beyond the corporate values and know them better.

Most carriers own fleets of trucks, so the challenge is to align your personal values with theirs. The idea here is to try and understand how they grew to where they are today. What values have kept them in the industry for so long? Besides, carriers are always in talks with each other, so you can rest assured that you will be a subject of discussion with a good relationship from time to time.

8. **Generate leads from everyday products**

Look around you. All the products you use were once delivered by trucks: Carriers transported cars, furniture, the laptop, or phone you are using right now. You can find carriers using this analogy. First, you need to find out where products used frequently around you were manufactured and how they move from the manufacturing plant to the end-user.

Another way to go about this is thinking about your most recent purchases. Try and track down the bill of lading and any other useful shipping information and documents. This should give you the names of carriers. You will have successfully created a database of local carriers that you can work with. Find out how they run their business, how far they can go, and from there, you can consider using their experience and expertise in the field to expand your brokerage firm.

9. **Online search**

Having an online presence is something every business is thinking about today. You probably have this written down in your business plan. Many carriers are embracing this concept and are getting websites and active social media pages. Unfortunately, the uptake is relatively slow, especially since most carriers operate as independent contractors or small businesses; hence, complete disregard for the benefits of integrating technology into their business operations. A quick online search for carriers in your region will be useful. Apart from that, you can also see their reviews online.

10. Understand the freight

It is easier to convince carriers to haul cargo for you when you both understand the contents and any unique requirements for it. Some carriers are strict on the kind of cargo they can haul, either because of personal reasons or their equipment can only allow them to handle that limit. You have an easier time getting a carrier onboard if you can describe the freight properly.

To do this, ensure the shipper gives you all the information you need. This will also make it easier to qualify carriers for cargo faster. Whenever you have urgent or crucial freight coming in, you are certain about the carriers who are comfortable transporting it and on time. You will also have a shortlist of carriers with the most competitive rates and those who can transport fragile cargo.

11. Mastering upload settings

Before you look for carriers, you need to understand how uploads are handled. Carriers do not like being stranded, waiting for days for cargo to be prepared. Each day the truck is not hauling cargo, they lose money. For this reason, ensure you can organize quick turnarounds before getting a carrier, such that when you contact them, the load is all set and ready to move.

12. Consider other modes of transportation

The transport industry is not limited to truckload carrier services. While this is common, there are other options, like rail and air freight too. Keeping your options open, you can also try and establish relations with carriers in those avenues.

Eventually, your success in this industry will come down to how well you can coordinate the needs and requirements of carriers, shippers and consignees. This is an industry where critical cargo comes up from time to time, so you must also learn to respond to them quickly.

By offering multiple ways of moving freight, you give customers more options, which translates to price flexibility from one point. Besides, when you offer these and other services, customers believe you are a growth-oriented broker, which means an opportunity to grow with your business. This way, your customers can take advantage of the opportunity to use intermodal conversion methods, saving more in the process. They can use more capacity in one mode when other modes are at full capacity.

What Do Customers Look For?

Now that we know how to find shippers and carriers, how do you keep them on your books for a long time? There are small and large brokerage firms in the market, and they all angle for the same pool of customers all the time. You can only offer quality brokerage services when you understand the needs of your customers. With this in mind, we will look at the factors that influence the customers' decisions and what they look for in a broker. This can become a checklist that helps you make sure you can meet the customer's needs.

Shippers use freight brokers for these key reasons:

1. **Capacity building -** this way, they don't need to add carriers to their routing schedule. They bring you onboard to simplify their routing schedule. In the process, you ease pressure on their routing schedule such that the shipper can handle more demand without having to expand their routing schedule.

2. **Ease of transportation -** you become an extension of their managed transportation services, streamlining the link between the logistics service provider and the shipper.

Bearing these in mind, the following are some of the things that shippers hope to find before they bring their business to you:

1. **Fully licensed broker**

You must have the required licenses to operate in the freight industry. From time to time, you will come across people purporting to offer brokerage services when, in the real sense, they do not have the necessary licenses. Do not take shortcuts. Ensure you are licensed by FMCSA (customers can verify your license online).

2. **Stable finances**

Shippers are interested in your financial standing to gauge whether you have the capacity to do business with them. No matter how long you have been in the industry, brokers come and go, and each time a broker winds up operations, shippers are left stranded and have to incur the costs and inconveniences of looking for a new broker.

Financial stability is also important to the shipper because if you ever close down, they bear the burden of paying carriers for the load delivered. This situation introduces the risk of double payment, including attorney fees where applicable. This is why shippers will run a credit check to ensure you are capable of handling their business.

Building on that, shippers also check to ensure you have the right insurance policies instead of their business operation. In particular, they look for contingent cargo and shipper's interest policies. The shipper's interest policy, for example, covers the cargo being transported, which is critical to safeguarding the shipper's business interests. Note that shippers can also verify whether your insurance payments are up to date.

3. **Deductible**

Depending on the nature of the shipper's cargo, some deductibles can be too high such that small brokers cannot comfortably handle them. Let's assume you just started your brokerage business. Processing deductibles of $30,000 would be a tall order, especially if your bank cannot assist.

4. **Vetting carriers**

Shippers are also interested in finding out how you vet carriers. This is important because you are just the intermediary. Ideally, the carriers you choose work for the shipper. Some of the industry's biggest brokers have thousands of carriers on contract, and they have a way of monitoring them.

Some of the issues shippers will need assurances about include the number of approved and active shippers you have on contract, your approval process, whether they are insured, how you monitor and update changes to the carrier profiles and how frequently you do that.

How do you confirm carrier safety ratings? Do you have a policy in place for delisting carriers who breach your terms of engagement?

5. **Reputation matters**

Reputation is vital in this industry. Even if you are a new broker, you can create a buzz around your name. Network with, and get other experienced brokers to vouch for you. When customers are looking for a broker to handle their cargo, they come with the mindset of adding an employee to their company. This is where your reputation comes in.

One way of raising your profile is to join relevant trade associations. All the major brokers in the market belong to trade associations, so some customers take it as a red flag if you do not belong to any of them. Membership to these organizations carries some weight because of their vetting procedure. Before admission, they run background checks to determine whether you are fit to become a member. From there, you can engage in their activities and even use their logo on your website. The following are some of the associations you can join, which will boost your reputation:

- Intermodal Association of North America (IANA)
- Transportation Intermediaries Association (TIA)

Most customers will check your name on the association websites. This helps them determine your credibility, especially since some rogue brokers have association logos on their websites, yet they are not members.

6. Business footprint

Finally, shippers will always want to see your business footprint. These days, there is so much information you can search online about a business. Their contacts, address, business history, ratings and reviews are all available online. If you have a social media page, that's one of the first places customers will check.

Customers are skeptical of brokers who do not have an online presence. If you do not have the resources to set up a website or professional company emails, for example, it hurts your reputation. If you have a website, LinkedIn and other social media pages, make sure they are professionally done and managed. From your social media and blog posts, customers have an idea of your values and beliefs. If they align with how they run their businesses, you can expect they will reach out.

Now that you know what customers look for when they need brokerage services and how to find reliable shippers and carriers, try and implement the tips in your work and see your brokerage business grow from strength to strength.

Creating Quality Brokerage Business

To succeed in the brokerage business, you must create value and offer quality services. Think of the struggle you go through to bring new shippers on board and how much effort you put into finding the right carriers for their goods. You have to find ways of keeping customers happy so that your business can grow. Unhappy customers effectively damage your brand reputation, while happy customers recommend your brokerage services. Remember that bad news travels faster than good news and usually has a lasting impact on your business.

To create a quality business in the industry, whether you are a start-up broker or have been in the business for a while, you must first tap into all the networks you have for connections. The easiest way to get a reliable carrier for a shipment is to go through your database. Keep records for all the carriers you work with and note down any significant features about their services. This will reduce the duration of time you spend looking for carriers, especially when you have urgent cargo.

Organizations like the TIA are another place you can go for carrier connections. Apart from connections, you can also use this as an opportunity to learn best practices in the market, build relationships, and make use of resources available to brokers and shippers. Once you are a member of the TIA, you have access to amazing tools that can help you streamline the carrier selection process. Membership to this body also gives you access to a list of carriers who have since been flagged for fraudulent deeds. This can help you avoid losses by contracting an irresponsible carrier.

- **Load prices and carrier quality**

For quality business in this market, you get as much as you give. This is a principle that, in utmost good faith, encourages you to operate your brokerage business as diligently as you can. One of your objectives is probably to save as much as possible from the margins in terms of costs. Remember that every other party in the industry worries about margins, too. Do not let this cloud your judgment. If all you offer are low-paying loads, you can forget about getting high-quality carriers.

In this industry, word goes around so fast, and if you have a reputation for paying carriers too little, such a reputation will stay with you for a long time. The solution is to research and understand the prevailing market rate for different load types and offer carriers rates that are reasonable and acceptable within the market. Note that the freight brokerage business prices vary from time to time, so you must also revise your load rates accordingly.

Occasionally, you will come across some low-quality drivers working with some of the industry's top carrier companies. These are random outlier situations that are expected in any market. However, you can mitigate this risk by using load schedulers that verify their carrier credentials from time to time. Alternatively, you can also seek information from insurance service providers, the licensing authorities and check their safety scores.

- **Champion the change you want**

If you want to attract the best drivers in the market, you must also have a reputation for being a responsible and reliable broker. Give your drivers the same attention and care you would expect them to give you and your customers. If you conduct business with them in a logical and ethical manner, they will return the favor.

Unfortunately, many brokers mistreat carriers, yet they expect the carriers to treat them with respect. Think about the way you conduct business. Pay carriers on time, communicate instructions to them clearly, and talk to them with respect. If you make a commitment with a carrier, follow through on it. These are some of the incentives that make carriers look forward to working with you.

That being said, you should also go the extra mile and learn about the underlying rules of the transportation and transport industry. Just because you connect a carrier to the shipper does not mean that you make them work like slaves for you. To be precise, go through the Hours of Service (HOS) regulations. This shows you the maximum number of hours a trucker should be driving, the recommended break limits, and the drivers' required sleep. Carriers haul so much dollar value in their trucks, and the last thing you want is loss from accidents because of a fatigued driver.

Besides, if you keep pushing carriers to work beyond the recommended hours contrary to the HOS regulations, you will soon find yourself on the wrong side of the law, and this might even cost you your license. As much as you want the cargo to arrive on time, it is also your responsibility to give the driver ample resources to protect other passengers and road users. Go through the delivery schedule and deadlines keenly and understand the requirements so that you do not assign carriers impossible delivery schedules. Not only will they struggle to meet those deadlines, but you also risk losing the customer because you committed to an impossible schedule. Yet, you could have easily discussed it with them and rescheduled the delivery accordingly.

- **Trust and reliability**

Be an honest freight broker. Brokers in every industry are often treated with contempt because people see the worst traits of middlemen in them. Indeed, you cannot miss a few rotten apples in every industry. You should, however, set yourself aside and abide by a strict code of conduct. For example, do not double broker a carrier.

Double brokering is a situation where the carrier, who might also be a freight broker, agrees to transport a load from another broker. Unknown to the legitimate broker, the carrier then brokers the load to another carrier. This is an illegal practice. Be as transparent as possible when conducting business with carriers and shippers. Engaging in illegal practices like double brokerage will only leave you knee-deep in legal disputes. At the same time, you earn a reputation in the eyes of shippers and carriers as an untrustworthy and unreliable broker. Such a reputation is hard to shake off.

Those who engage in such activities usually have some cash flow problems they try to overcome by circumventing the rules. Suppose you find yourself in such a position. In that case, there are many financial service providers you can work with who will offer accounts receivable products and handle carrier payments on your behalf.

Chapter 7
The Legalities and Formalities

As an intermediary, you handle shipments across state lines and, for that reason, all the broker authority businesses are operated under the purview of the FMCSA. At this point, you already know the prerequisites to become a freight broker, from obtaining your operating license to getting a surety bond and so on. The next step is to understand the legal status of your business. Away from the daily activities that keep you in business, there are legal requirements that you must meet to operate legally. Compliance is mandatory, without which you risk losing business, heavy fines, or even jail term.

Before you start your brokerage firm, you must decide the type of business entity you wish to establish. This is important because when you register the business, it becomes a separate legal entity from yourself. As a separate legal entity, your business assumes an identity as a person, such that it can sue and be sued, enter into contracts with other parties and so on.

There are different business models under which you can register your brokerage firm. Knowledge of each of them helps you determine the most suitable for your business. This is important because the type of business you register determines how you file tax returns. The last thing you want is the IRS on your case. Let's look at the common types of business under which you can register your brokerage firm below:

Sole Proprietorship

In this structure, you are the owner of an unincorporated brokerage firm. You pay personal income tax on all the profits earned from your brokerage firm. This is one of the easiest businesses to register and operate because there are no regulations. Since you don't necessarily need a separate trade or business name, many sole proprietors operate under their own names. As your business grows, however, you can convert the sole proprietorship to an LLC.

The main difference between a sole proprietorship and a corporation is that you do not create a separate legal entity. For this reason, you are responsible for all liabilities incurred and lawsuits entered into by the business. This means that your brokerage firm's debts and obligations are your personal responsibility, too.

Ease of creation, low cost of registration and maintenance, and the pass-through advantage make sole proprietorship a good option for a startup. That being said, you will usually have to raise startup capital on your own. Besides, it is not easy to get financing from established financiers like banks or obtain a credit line. There is also an unlimited liability, which leaves your personal affairs exposed if you cannot honor your business liabilities and debts. Many businesses start as sole proprietors, but you can transition into a limited liability entity as they grow.

For the purpose of taxation, where applicable, you might be liable for income tax, self-employment tax, estimated tax, social security and medicare taxes, withholding tax, federal unemployment tax, excise tax, and file information returns if you made payments in the course of your operation to non-employees.

Partnerships

A partnership is an agreement between two or more people to operate and manage a business, sharing profits in the process. There are many partnership agreements under which you can register your brokerage firm. In business partnerships, profits and liabilities are shared among the partners equally or under any other sharing agreement entered into by the partners. This is true in partnerships where some partners have limited liability. There are three main types of partnerships you can enter into:

1. General partnership
2. Limited partnership
3. Limited liability partnership

In a general partnership, everyone shares profits and liabilities equally. All partners are personally liable for the debts and obligations entered into by the partnership. Profits and losses are shared equally or according to instructions spelled out in the partnership agreement.

Professionals commonly enter into limited liability partnerships. These include doctors, lawyers, architects and accountants. The nature of their limited liability is such that if one of the partners incurs legal damages for malpractice or any other reason, the other partners' assets are not affected.

Limited partnerships are a blend of general partnerships and limited liability partnerships. In this operation, you must have at least one general partner. This partner assumes full personal liability for the debts of the partnership. You must also have at least one silent partner whose liability is limited to the amount they invested, but they do not take part in the partnership's active running.

You must file an annual information return reporting your income, deductions, profits and losses from running the freight business. However, according to the Internal Revenue Code (Chapter 1, subchapter K), instead of paying income tax, partnerships share the profits or losses among partners, who in turn report their share on their personal tax returns.

That being said, if you operate the freight business as a partnership, you might file the following forms:

1. Annual return of partnership income
2. Employment taxes including social security and medicare taxes
3. Excise tax

On the other hand, the individuals who make up the partnership might file the following forms:

1. Income tax
2. Self-employment tax
3. Estimated tax
4. International tax

For taxation, partners in a partnership are not considered employees, hence the self-employment tax. On the same note, if you want to register a freight brokerage, it might be better to register as a partnership instead of a corporation because of favorable tax obligations. For example, profits earned in corporations and dividends paid to shareholders are taxed. This is pretty much double taxation. This does not happen to partnership profits.

Corporations

Corporations are legal entities, distinct and separate from the owners. The entity registered as a corporation assumes all the rights and responsibilities that you have as an individual. This means that they can give and receive loans, sue and be sued, enter contracts, own property and other assets, pay taxes, and hire employees. Legally, a corporation becomes a person.

One of the highlights of corporations is that their liability is limited. With this, shareholders earn profits paid through stock appreciation and dividends but cannot be held liable for the entity's debts. This is the most important feature of corporations.

This entity is created by shareholders, with common stock working towards common goals. Your corporation can have one or more shareholders, depending on the nature of the business.

Corporations deduct taxable income in the same way that sole proprietors do. However, the corporation can also get special deductions. Corporation profits are taxed when the business earns them. The profits are also taxed when shareholders receive them as dividends. This is what we mentioned earlier as double taxation.

S Corporations

S corporations are also referred to as S subchapter entities. This is a special type of corporation that is set up based on unique Internal Revenue Code laws. Under this guide, if you set up the brokerage firm as an S corporation with less than 100 shareholders, you enjoy all the benefits of incorporation but get taxed as a partnership. Therefore, instead of suffering double taxation, S corporations can pass income to shareholders in the same way partnerships do.

Since all the profits, losses, credits and deductions are passed to shareholders, they are reported in their personal tax returns and assessed at income tax rates. However, S corporations are still liable for taxes on passive income. To register your brokerage firm as an S corporation, you must meet the following conditions:

1. Register as a domestic corporation
2. Have 100 shareholders or less
3. All shareholders own only one class of stock.
4. The corporation must not have been registered as any of the corporations ineligible to operate as an S corporation, such as insurance companies and financial institutions.

Once you register your company, you might only be liable to pay income tax, employment taxes, excise taxes and estimated tax. Registering your firm as an S corporation gives it credibility, especially with suppliers, potential customers and other investors because of the nature of the commitment to the business.

Since it passes taxables to shareholders, you save a lot of money that would have otherwise gone to corporate tax. Such savings are useful to startups because you can divert them to other critical aspects of the business like marketing.

For all the benefits, you must be careful when registering your brokerage firm as an S corporation. The IRS takes a particular interest in these firms because some entities try to avoid payroll taxes by disguising salaries as distributions to shareholders.

Limited Liability Company (LLC)

This is a business structure whose owners are not liable for the company's liabilities or debts. An LLC is basically a crossbreed of a corporation and a sole proprietorship or partnership. The limited liability clause of an LLC is similar to that of a corporation, but at the same time, the shareholders are taxed in the flow-through manner that happens in partnerships. Since LLCs are registered under state statutes, there might be different requirements in your state, so you should always check the requirements with the state.

Owners in an LLC are referred to as members, and unlike S corporations, there is no restriction on membership. Therefore, you can have corporations, individuals, foreign entities, or even other LLCs as members of your brokerage LLC. On the same note, while S corporation membership is capped at 100,

LLCs membership is unlimited. You can also register your brokerage LLC as a single-member in many states if you wish to remain the sole owner.

For the purpose of taxation, the IRS treats your LLC as a partnership, corporation or a disregarded entity as part of your tax returns, depending on the options you choose when registering the company.

Other than the liability protection, which is the main reason business owners register companies, LLCs are easier to set up than corporations and allow you more flexibility. However, note that if you do not honor your legal requirements as an LLC or if there's proof of fraud, creditors can come after individual LLC members. Depending on the state laws applicable in your jurisdiction, you can dissolve the LLC if one of the members is dead or declared bankrupt. This is different from corporations, which exist in perpetuity.

Registering Your Business

Having looked at the different business structures, you can then move on to register your business accordingly. Choosing an appropriate business structure is essential because it will determine how you file tax returns and how much tax you pay. Generally, you don't want to spend so much of your earnings on taxes, so think about the business structure options, and choose the most appropriate one. If in doubt, you can always talk to an accountant or an attorney to help you evaluate your options.

1. **Application to the authorities**

Next, you will file your application with the relevant authorities. This industry's authority is the Federal Motor Carrier Safety Administration (FMCSA), a branch of the US Department of Transportation. They enforce safety regulations and oversee interstate commerce. Generally, it takes around four weeks to receive your authority once you submit the duly filled forms.

2. **Choose a process agent**

This will be the representative to whom legal papers can be addressed if anyone raises a court proceeding against you or a carrier relevant to your business. Since you handle cargo across multiple states, you must nominate a process agent in every state where you have an office or where you do business. Since it might be difficult to raise such an agent in all states, you can opt for blanket coverage to assign a process agent in all states within the country. Besides, you are in this business for growth, and in the transport and logistics industry, you will pretty much be serving the entire country.

3. **Organize a trust fund or surety bond**

We mentioned the importance of a surety bond or trust fund earlier in the book. It is a mandatory requirement for all freight brokers to protect shippers and carriers' interests in case you are unable to honor your contractual obligations. Visit your insurance agent and discuss this with them. It is through them that you can fill and file the necessary documents with the FMCSA.

4. **Business registration**

You must apply for the Unified Carrier Registration and pay the annual fee, which is usually in the range of $60–$80 a year.

With all these covered, you are ready to operate as a licensed freight broker. However, remember that states might have different requirements regarding the freight brokerage business. Therefore, make sure you check with state agents and authorities to ensure you have all that is required to operate in the state.

Compliance Requirements

The Code of Federal Regulations (CFR), Part 371 - Brokers of Property, spells out all the compliance requirements that freight brokers must adhere to. The general compliance requirements for brokers are as follows:

1. **Maintaining transaction records**

Under the CFR, you must maintain detailed records of all business transactions for at least three years. Some of the details covered by this statute include names and contact details of consignors, carriers, bill of lading, and the amount earned in return for brokerage services. These records are kept and open for review by any party to transactions involving your brokerage firm.

2. **Avoid misrepresentation**

You have a legal obligation not to misrepresent yourself as a carrier or offer a carrier's services when in the real sense, you are registered as a broker. All your marketing and advertising approaches must explicitly state that you offer brokerage services, not carrier services. Apart from that, you cannot offer or perform services in the industry under any other name apart from that which is duly licensed and registered with the FMCSA.

3. **Carrier charges**

You cannot charge carriers for services in which you have an interest in or own the cargo being hauled by the carrier. This statute also applies to situations where your business owns or is owned by a shipper, giving you legal obligations to control the cargo. On the same note, your brokerage firm cannot give or offer anything of value to shippers other than marketing materials of inexpensive value.

4. **Responsible accounting**

All business revenues and expenditures must be accounted for in your accounting books, especially when they are derived from other business forms other than the freight brokerage services. Revenue and expenditure related to the brokerage service should be distinct from additional revenues and expenses. In case they are shared, you must allocate them equitably.

5. **Annual bond renewal**

One of the most important compliance requirements for brokerage firms is to ensure you renew your annual bond on time. It seems like a simple thing, but considering the number of brokerage firms submitting renewals for approval, you can expect delays from time to time.

Apart from delays, you can also make the innocent mistake of forgetting to renew your bond on time, as do other freight brokers in the market. Note that the FMCSA is within its mandate to suspend your brokerage license without the renewal. To avoid this, sureties will generally send you renewal reminders 60 days before yours expires, and in some cases, earlier. To prevent unfortunate mishaps and risk losing your license, renew your bond as soon as you receive the surety's reminder. This gives them sufficient time to process the application and forward to FMCSA.

The Transportation Management System (TMS)

A transportation management system (TMS) is a logistics platform that leverages technology to enable you to plan, execute and optimize the movement of incoming and outgoing cargo. Such a system is also useful in ensuring all the carriers and cargo are compliant, and you receive all the necessary documentation regarding the undersigned shipment. By design, a TMS is an important extension of a supply chain management system.

One of the key roles of the TMS is to bring visibility to your daily brokerage operations by supporting compliance, ensuring freight is received delivered on time and streamlining the shipping process. An efficient TMS makes it easier for you to optimize and manage your brokerage business

's transportation aspect.

As an essential cog in supply chain management, they affect all logistics processes, which translates to high customer satisfaction because of efficient transport planning and execution. Satisfied customers mean more sales and business growth. The following are some of the opportunities you enjoy with a good TMS:

- Allows you to update cargo to the system
- Processes invoices

- Searches for available and relevant transport
- Real-time cargo and fuel tax tracking
- Updating cargo status
- Route planning and logistics
- Accounting

Benefits of Freight Broker Software

Given all the programs available in the market at the moment, you might be spoilt for choice. Once you know the key features to look for, you can purchase the best program to support your brokerage business. The following are some of the main benefits you will enjoy when using any of the top-rated programs in the market:

- **Shipping calculator**

A good program shows you upfront on what it costs to deliver cargo from one point to the next. This helps you plan accordingly when talking to carriers and shippers. The freight shipping calculator considers the requirements for transporting cargo from point to point, including the type of transport available and suitable for the underlying cargo, type of cargo, and conditions necessary for transport.

- **Carrier selection**

With so many carriers available at any given time, you should be able to narrow down your choices based on carrier suitability for the cargo. Some of the factors taken into consideration include the route, type and volume of cargo. A good program allows you to create filters to help you select the best carrier.

- **Benefits of consolidation**

As much as you are in the business of connecting carriers and shippers, you must also try to reduce overheads in the process. One way of doing this is to consolidate cargo where possible. You can reduce unnecessary expenses by consolidating similar items for a carrier.

- **Choosing the best route**

When choosing an ideal route for delivery, many factors come into play. Things like the fuel cost, distance, and road condition do not just determine the best route, but it also affects the delivery timeline and the cost. Good programs consider such factors and help you optimize and select the best delivery route.

- **Real-time cargo tracking**

Everyone involved in the delivery process is always at ease when they know where the cargo is at any given time as long as it is in transit. The shipper's concern is the safety of their cargo, while your concern is the carrier's safety and the delivery of the cargo. This is where real-time tracking comes in. This allows you to track cargo all the time and on any route. With updates at regular intervals, you can convey the estimated arrival time to the shipper if anything happens on the carrier's route and alert them of any emergencies or delays that are beyond yours or the carrier's control. This level of transparency will not just give the shipper peace of mind. It will also build their trust in you and your brokerage services.

Choosing the Best Software

From the benefits discussed above, you need quality brokerage software if you are to succeed in this industry and become a reliable broker. Such programs help you work faster, efficiently manage customer shipment and expectations, and in the process, earn more money by eliminating unnecessary costs.

There are two ways of going about this. You can consult a team of experts to build a TMS unique to your brokerage firm or obtain a license for one of the top programs available in the market. The first option is more expensive because developers have to build an app from scratch. It will also take more time. Other than that, there are added costs for maintenance and updates, and since the program is unique to your business, you might struggle if you encounter bugs or problems that the developer had not factored in.

Buying a license, however, makes more sense. There is always a team of developers working round the clock to manage and maintain the program. Here are some tips to help you choose the best freight brokerage program:

- **Go for brokerage software**

There are many programs in the market, but not all of them are ideal for your business. You want something custom-made for freight brokers. Many of the programs you find are a complete bundle that includes features useful to carriers, shippers and fleets. The extra add-ons are necessary for you, but you will still pay for them.

Besides, with all the functions you don't need, the program becomes too difficult to learn, and it's even more challenging to integrate into your operation. The best option is to look for programs built explicitly for freight brokers. Alternatively, contact a software developer to create one unique to your needs, though this is generally pricier.

- **Flexible software**

You are in the business for growth. Any software you purchase for your business must support this cause, too. It is wise to look for programs whose functions can scale up as your operation grows. Apart from scaling up, it should be flexible to integrate into other services or customize it to suit your needs.

- **Data security**

The last thing you want to be vulnerable to in the business world today is a data breach, especially when you consider the nature and commercial value of the cargo you handle. Bearing this in mind, talk to an expert on proper data security and storage. You can store data on a server, offline, or with a professional service provider.

Whichever you choose, you must still conduct regular system audits to ensure your data is safe, and more importantly, follow all the guidelines necessary to protect your and your customers' data safe. Note that irresponsible data handling leading to a severe breach will not just damage customer trust in your brokerage firm. You might also suffer hefty fines and penalties.

- **Easy to understand**

Choose a program that is easy to understand. You don't want to spend a lot of money on training, especially when you scale the business and hire a team to assist you. If you are unable to understand the program, chances are high that your team might also struggle. Besides, if the program is too complicated, you might leave yourself exposed to data breaches. Apart from training, you should also purchase a product whose developers offer regular updates. You don't want to be left with a program that has not received updates in a long time or one that might be discontinued in the near future.

Top Freight Brokerage Software

While there are many programs in the market, the secret is to find one that offers features you can use immediately or in the foreseeable future. Other functions you can consider include carrier portal, management, generating quotes, database and dispatch management, scheduling and trip logs. You cannot find all these functions in one program.

Some of the functions might also be available but not work the way you expect them to. An acceptable trade-off is to find a program that meets most of your needs. Below are some of the top freight brokerage programs you can get in the market:

Aljex: Starts at $290 a month

Key features:

- You can control access and visibility to agents, protecting sensitive information
- Monitor shipment in real-time
- Monitor prices and compare with historical rates
- View dispatch on maps
- Secure cloud backups and hosting
- Easy document management and imaging
- Automated invoice payment and freight billing

Loadpilot: Starts at $99 a month

Key features:

- Integrated accounting system
- Supports international shipment handling
- Can integrate into load boards
- Job and load tracking
- Supports multimodal transportation and management

Truckstop: Starts at $ a75 month

Key features:

- You can add an unlimited number of users
- Simple invoice handling
- Easy to create a bill of lading
- Imprint your logo on all company documents
- Integrate with QuickBooks
- Supports sales management tools

3plsystems: Comes with a free demo. Full pricing upon consultation

Key features:

- Supports carrier selection
- Includes sales management tools
- Customers can track shipments on the portal

- Integrates with leading accounting suites like QuickBooks
- You can create sales quotes and track shipments to each account

AscendTMS: Starts at $69 a month, per user

Key features

- No license, setup, training, or maintenance fees
- Tech support available all-round the clock
- Free carrier and driver verification
- You can check credit scores
- Access to shipper directory
- Automated carrier payments
- Integrate into QuickBooks

Rose Rocket: Starts at $99 a month

Key features

- Minimal data entry involved
- Manage multi-carrier and multi-movement orders
- Supports LTL distribution
- Manage route and shipment expenses
- Automated invoice processing

Axon: Starts at $99 a month

Key features

- Quick invoice processing
- Receive fuel reports instantly
- Real-time integration into accounting suites
- Fleet management services
- Offers transport management services

Tailwind: Starts at $99 a month per user

Key features

- Settle driver and carrier payments instantly
- Text messaging services
- Quote and order system
- Customize your business logo
- Includes a customer and vendor database
- Payables and receivables account management
- Integrate into QuickBooks Online

Q7 Trucking Software: Starts at $20 a month

Key features

- Supports truckload and brokerage dispatch
- Fleet management
- Fuel and mileage management
- Payroll and accounting services
- Supports LTL dispatch

Logitude: Starts at $39 a month

Key features

- Freight forwarding management
- Prepare financial statements
- Automated invoice handling
- Manage shipment quotes seamlessly
- Personalization functions for all business sizes

CloudWadi: Starts at $35 a month

Key features

- Support online request handling
- Custom clearance services
- Manage accounting and prepare financial statements
- Automated invoice handling
- Includes a CRM
- Real-time cargo tracking

Logistically: Starts at $300 a month

Key features

- Manage sales online
- Supports accounting services
- Easy rate negotiation
- Support truckload and LTL management

- Customize to suit your business needs

FreightPath: Starts at $25 a month

Key features

- Scalable according to your business needs
- Easy collaboration with drivers and shippers
- Customize business documents with your color scheme and logo
- In-built invoice support

Chapter 8
Grow Your Business With Smart Marketing

You have realized, by now, how big the freight brokerage business is. As long as the world keeps spinning on its axis, cargo is always moving from one place to the other. This means that there is an endless demand, and to fulfill that demand, there will always be many freight brokers in the market. Whether or not you are new to the industry, there is plenty of fish in the sea for everyone. Essentially, the business is between the shipper and the carrier, but you are an important middleman whose services make work easier for everyone involved. With the competition in this industry, you must be sharp at marketing your services.

The industry has been transforming over the years. Today, there is so much more technology in play than there was a decade ago, which proves the evolution of freight brokerage over the years. If you are getting into the freight brokerage business today, you must think about lead generation and digitizing your enterprise.

As much as networking and connections earned through personal relationships in the industry were, and still are, useful in winning contracts, you have to do more. Connections are an excellent tool in your arsenal within this industry, but without structuring your business for modern society and the modern customer, you are bound to fail.

You must work towards finding new and more effective ways of reaching out to customers and keeping them satisfied. Large brokerage firms are taking advantage of technology to widen their market share, and if you do not follow suit and align your brokerage firm with the changing times, you stand to lose a lot. So, how do you use marketing techniques to build a resilient freight forwarding business? The answer is in lead generation.

Lead generation is a marketing process where you raise awareness and interest in your brokerage products and services. The end goal is to obtain new customers and keep the old ones happy. Lead generation makes use of digital channels for capturing, qualifying, and converting leads. To get you started, we will discuss some practical marketing methods that will get you closer to the results you yearn for.

This chapter will delve into effective marketing strategies that will help you drive sales and boost your reputation among carriers and shippers. Marketing is key to your success in this business, so devote as much time and resources as you can to it, and the results will be worth your investment. Below are useful tips to help you create quality marketing content for your freight brokerage firm:

Originality

Given the number of brokers in the market, you cannot take chances with copied content. You are selling yourself as a brand, so you must come up with original marketing material. True, you can borrow ideas from elsewhere, but the final product you present to customers should be unique and show your brand in the best light.

Regarding originality, you must also curate marketing content that is relevant to the industry. There is so much to work within this case. The industry keeps growing, and one of the areas you can shed light on is the impact of technology trends and how they shape the future of freight forwarding. Customers will not just come to you for business. They will also come to you because you seem knowledgeable and they can learn a thing or two from you.

You can also borrow from several datasets available in the market and make your own analysis. This makes for good reading on your blog if you have a website. You can also share links to your social media pages for further interaction. You might even find some of the industry's top players commenting on such content, and when such authority figures reach out, you are doing something right.

Customer-Centric Content

While the emphasis is on creating original content, you must also make sure it is geared towards the customer's needs and interests. Let's say your new target is shippers in the retail sector. There is always something new in the retail industry that you can create content around. The idea here is to keep customers interested in your content and convert that to business leads.

Another opportunity that many freight brokers miss from time to time is to leverage their marketing efforts on world events—for example, the World Cup. Research and find out what people need in sporting retail outlets. Find out the challenges that shippers and carriers have in terms of delivering on their end of the supply chain, and address such in your marketing content. Do not just sell stories; sell a call to action. Once shippers read your blog post, for example, encourage them to get in touch for a quote to deliver their World Cup merchandise on time.

Online Marketing

Creating unique content gives you an upper hand in marketing your brokerage firm because your material becomes the springboard for all your marketing efforts. First, ensure you have a professional website. Online audiences are big on aesthetics, so you cannot take that for granted. Once you have content on your website, you can share it with the relevant parties.

From the moment you enter the industry, start building a mailing list. Keep emails of all customers you work with and add them to your email marketing list. The beauty of email marketing is that you are always in charge, and you can send customers fresh content whenever you have it ready.

Another option that many people use today is podcasting. Podcasts have recently become popular in every other niche. There is always someone running a podcast about something dear to them. You can discuss issues in-depth through podcasts and explain them better than you would have done using written content. It is about owning and controlling a narrative.

Through podcasts, you can also reach out to some of the industry's authority figures and discuss some of the current issues affecting freight brokers, carriers, and shippers. You can talk about the impact of new regulations or legislation on the bottom-line for industry stakeholders. This approach gives you credibility and raises your profile.

Finally, the mother of them all—social media. Currently, any credible business must have an online presence on social media. Twitter and LinkedIn, in particular, are great assets for businesses. You can use the platforms to engage users and drive leads to your brokerage website. You can use social media to establish relationships with customers. From your conversations, encourage them to join your email marketing list.

Understand Customer Needs

All players in the freight and logistics industry have varying needs in relation to your brokerage services. While some need customer clearance, others need reefer containers or trucking services. To market your brokerage effectively, you must understand what your customers need. This way, you can offer them a good value proposition by showing them the benefits of working with you.

To understand customers, talk to some of your current customers. Learn their purchasing process and use that to guide them towards signing up for your services. Another option is to use Google Analytics. This is a free, useful tool whose metrics offer incredible insight into your website's customer behavior and interaction.

Without facing them directly, you can also learn from competitors and understand how they keep their heads up in the industry. This can shed light on their lead generation approaches, which you can also try out.

Today, there are many discussion forums from where you can interact with all kinds of shippers, carriers, and freight brokers. In such places, you learn about their challenges, fears, and everything else in the business. Note down the complaints and do something about them. Present your brokerage business as the solution to their problems.

Understanding customer needs is key to creating a customer persona through which you can understand the ideal customer and how to reach out to them. This information will also be useful in our next point.

Create a Professional Website

It is one thing to create a website and a whole different ball game to create a professional and effective one. A professional website must deliver an incredible user experience for customers. Ideally, you want people to come to your website and spend more time on it. This is where the user experience is important. It helps you to add value to customers. People generally come to your website looking for solutions. Whether they need to move cargo or get a quote, their experience on your website should be smooth and streamlined, or they will never return.

A good user experience also helps to market your brand. It gives carriers, shippers and other users an idea of the kind of business you operate, and more importantly, gives them confidence that you can handle their freight forwarding needs.

Lead generation is essential in converting online traffic to contracts, and user experience is an integral part of that. An engaging website coupled with a well-thought-out buyer journey is the boost your marketing strategy needs.

Work on Your Content Strategy

You have come across the words SEO at some point. SEO, when done properly, will also boost your visibility online. It should be one of the elements of your content strategy. It is about planning, creating and managing engaging content. You can use SEO strategies in your infographics, videos, blogs and any other content you produce online.

Search engines appreciate SEO-friendly content and rank them well, giving you a wider reach to customers whose intention is to do business with you. You can also use different SEO tools to get insight into search keywords that customers use frequently and use those keywords to your advantage.

Even if you are new to the industry, you can learn from your competitors by analyzing their website and the keywords people use to find them, informing you of the kind of information that interests customers.

An excellent example of a content strategy that adds value is to post content about relevant news in the industry, breaking news, guides, how-to articles, or any other type of content that your customers will enjoy. Even with a good strategy, you must also make sure you produce quality content to bring customers closer to contracting you.

Market Your Strengths

Advertising your business as a freight brokerage service is not enough to convince customers to do business with you. Instead, go the extra mile and highlight the benefits of using your brokerage services. For example, one broker will offer affordable and unbeatable rates to shippers who sign up and make their first transaction in one week. This works, but it is not convincing because the user cannot quantify affordable and unbeatable value. Instead, you can offer a 30% discount to customers who sign up and make their transactions within one week. Anyone who reads the second offer will instantly do the math and tell how much they save if they use your brokerage service.

An easy way to do this is to list all the services you offer and its benefit. Note that your customers are constantly bombarded with offers as big as the market is, so be careful not to offer the same things as everyone else. Be creative and make your offers valuable.

Buyer Journey Stages

Your rates might be attractive and bring customers to your website, but what moves them from the website to your accounting books is your knowledge of the customer's journey. The first step is to ensure there are many contact points with potential customers. The customer journey is a three-step process as follows:

1. Top of the funnel - This is the stage where people seek answers through blogs, eBooks, whitepapers and any other content they find online.

2. Middle ground - In this stage, potential customers evaluate information by performing in-depth research. They review product demos, webinars, review case studies and so on.

3. Bottom of the funnel - It is at this point that you offer a lasting solution. You get customers to make a purchase. This is where you offer incentives, coupons, or free consultations.

Once you master this consumer journey process, you can gradually use it to influence the content you create and guide users progressively from the top to the bottom channel.

Call to Action (CTA)

A call to action is a subtle prompt for an immediate response from users. CTAs should be placed strategically so that they don't look out of place, or it doesn't feel like you are ambushing or coercing customers into making a decision. CTAs help in confirming conversions. You can create an incredible blog post and attract a lot of traffic, but if, at the end of it, you do not encourage the customers to do something, that effort and attention will go to waste.

You have come across CTAs when browsing your favorite websites online. They exist in many forms, and the most effective ones usually show a popup when you do something. For example, if you were scrolling down a webpage and you suddenly go for the close (x) button, you will get a popup asking you to sign up for the newsletter or not to go away and miss a 50% discount offer.

CTAs are effective, but how you place them makes them even more useful. You can use them as hyperlinks within your content. Traditionally, most people place them in the sidebar or footer of their webpages, but these do not usually have good results. The best option is to study the market and learn the best practices for using CTAs and apply them to your website. The thing about CTAs is that there is never one method that cuts across the board. Things change all the time, and to succeed with them, you must be ready to experiment and find a good blend that complements the website UX.

Quality Landing Pages

All the marketing you engage in should lead users to a professional landing page. Once you identify the most efficient CTAs and how to work them into the website UX, cap it off with an amazing landing page. A good landing page should encourage users to subscribe to the services you offer, submit their contact information in exchange for something, message you for clarification, or request a quote.

A compelling landing page should have a convincing title, followed by a concise message about what you expect from users. If you have a submit button, it should be visible and, more importantly, if you have more than one offer, they should all have dedicated landing pages.

Perform A/B Testing

All the marketing tips above will help you make some progress in getting attention to your website. However, it does not end there. The final step is to learn how to perform A/B testing. A/B testing is simply a process of comparing two pages to identify the difference in customer engagement. It is a controlled experiment to identify outliers and understand the reason for them.

When comparing two web pages, you might realize that affect conversion rates are the different placement of the CTA buttons, the overall layout of the webpage, colors used on the page, or even media content uploaded on the site. The idea behind A/B testing is to make sure that your website is always optimized for the best results, both for your marketing needs and the customer's value proposition.

Cold Calling

Cold calling is a marketing technique that is often looked down upon by many experts in the field, yet it is still one of the most effective tactics, especially in the freight brokerage business. At some point in your brokerage career, you have had to call a stranger and tried to convince them to get something you have, which you are not sure they want.

Cold calling requires confidence and, in the freight business, you cannot do without it. You are pretty much soliciting attention and business from potential customers who were not necessarily looking forward to or expecting your call. While most of it involves calling potential customers, you can also make a surprise visit in person.

It is an incredibly effective approach for a small business whose target audience is small but well-defined. The idea is to look for paying customers for your freight business. First, you must know where to find shippers, for example, directories and shipper databases.

Establish a working profile for your target based on specific demographic units. By the time you call a customer or their company, you should have done your research on them. You should know what their business is about and some of the challenges they experience. This gives you an upper hand because you should be ready with solutions to their problems when they pick up. Cold calling is pretty much an impromptu interview.

You must be organized and ready with a script. Preparing a script helps you control the narrative and the entire conversation. This makes it easier to lead the customer and get answers to all the questions you need. Even though your script will work, you must tweak it from time to time while still delivering quality results. The conversation starters, for example, cannot be the same all the time. You might learn the hard way that it is not easy to use the same line on a shipper in New York that you used on someone in Wisconsin.

Now, before you cold call someone, you must understand that they do not expect your call. Therefore, there's a good chance that your call will be a nuisance to them. If they pick up, but you lack that confident, authoritative voice, you will lose that contact. Be keen on the hours you call and the number of times you call. You must be relaxed because some customers can tell when you are not comfortable, and your anxiety will lose you that business.

Unless you are asked to, do not try to sell the recipient anything. If they answer your call, your objective is to get them comfortable enough to talk about their challenges. This is how you gain insight into their business and the opportunities you can derive from them. If your prospect mentions something that has bugged them for a while, try and dig in deeper so that you understand the real nature of their struggles. The more you get them talking about their pain points, the more opportunities you will uncover to solve their problems.

There is always a chance that a shipper can turn things around and quiz you about your freight brokerage service, your business model, capacity and customers you currently serve. If this happens, be confident and pitch your business to them as competently as you can. If you have a good TMS program, you can track all this information and run it by the potential customer. Remind them that you have real-time tracking and can see where your transit cargo is at all times.

How do you make cold calling work for you? First, you must prepare a list of potential calls you will make. If you have been in the industry before in a different capacity, you can also start with your contact list. Since you are not new to the industry, you are in a better position to offer competitive rates because you already understand the logistics industry's ins and outs.

Another method of cutting down on costs is to optimize the destination transportation by connecting companies that might need consignments moved around the same destination. Say you are having a consignment dropped at some destination. Call them beforehand and let them know about it. At the same time, since you will have a mode of transport ready after dropping off the load, find out if they have any load to be picked. This method might not always be successful, but there are times when the company might even need to drop off their own load. By offering them the service at a discounted rate, you create a good rapport with the company. Persistence is key when dealing with such companies. They might not have something for you to move at first, but when you keep asking and offering to assist, you might get a once-off order, which is an opportunity you can turn into repeat business.

You are playing in the big leagues now, so ensure that you have a professional approach and give your brand a fitting outlook. Create professional brochures and business cards. Let people know you are starting a freight brokerage business and get your family, friends, and acquaintances to help you spread the word. All you need is a breakthrough into the industry, one contact that breaks the ice for you, and from there, you can grow your presence in the business using diligent business approaches.

Since this is a reputation and networking industry, you must also strive to make a name for yourself. Referrals from your customers always work like a charm. As long as word keeps spreading about your professional approach, individual and corporate shippers might soon start reaching out to enjoy similar benefits too.

The bottom line is that cold calling is an entirely legitimate way of trying to get business, but from time to time, the call comes in at an unexpected hour and might be a bother. Understanding the best practices for cold calling can help you go beyond these challenges. You will also come up with a logical and friendly way to contact potential customers. Cold calling is about patience, waiting until you have enough information on or from the customer before presenting your value proposition to them.

Marketing is a crucial part of the freight business. Most brokers who invest heavily in marketing generate quality traffic and from their conversion rates, they are able to improve their business models and grow. As much as you invest in different marketing approaches, you must also make sure that your business is well-positioned for the kind of transformation you are going after. This way, you will not be overwhelmed by the engagement and interaction you receive from potential customers online.

Conclusion

The market projections and economic outlook for the freight brokerage business are promising. Even in the aftermath of a global pandemic, there is so much to look forward to. As a freight broker, running a successful business means a burning desire to offer customers and business partners accurate, relevant and timely information about their business interests. In general, the industry has experienced many challenges in recent times, as has every industry in 2020. However, things are beginning to align and the growth potential for this industry is high.

Starting a business is a bold move that many people are willing to take, so the fact that you are thinking about it is a massive step in the right direction. As an entrepreneur, you learn to brace yourself for the unknown. There are many risks involved in business, but you find ways to mitigate them and navigate the turbulent tide.

This book teaches and empowers you to become not just a freight broker but an astute businessperson. Getting into the freight brokerage industry, you realize fast how close-knit the relations are, yet it is one of the world's largest industries. This is a testament to one reality—reputation is key to your success as a broker.

About reputation, you will soon realize that there are all kinds of participants in this industry. You will come across fraudulent carriers, impatient shippers, and other characters that might make you question your resolve and motivation to do business with them. Like every other business enterprise, this is nothing new. The secret is learning how to overcome such obstacles and run a profitable and credible freight brokerage business.

Just because you come across one or two people who are cutting corners and making it in the freight industry does not mean you should do the same. Unfortunately, many young entrepreneurs get into the market and are caught up in the allure of chasing quick riches. Before you know it, the law catches up, and you lose not just your good reputation, you also lose the business. You have to be patient and build your brokerage empire one brick at a time.

With all market indicators pointing towards steady growth in the brokerage industry, this is as good as any other time to set up your brokerage firm. While the global economy has slowed down in light of the coronavirus pandemic, it is worth mentioning that the freight industry is still operational. Naturally, there has been slow uptake in many parts of the world resulting in backlogs from time to time, but this is normal in the event of a global disruption of such a scale.

We comprehensively covered the requirements for setting up a freight brokerage business and with this information, you will have an easier time getting started. We also covered the market research and analysis on the freight brokerage business, highlighting the competitive advantage and the impact of disruptive technology in the market. This will give you a better head start going into the business because you already know what to do. An important highlight, in this case, is the fact that because of the technological benefits, you can now compete at the same level as some of the top brokerage firms in the industry.

Most recently, many industries have changed their mode of operation, with many sending employees to work from home. This is also a benefit you can realize in the brokerage industry. You do not necessarily have to show up at the loading docks in-person to ensure that carriers have the correct load. This can be organized from the comfort of your home. This way, you alert the carrier to pick up a consignment and deliver it to the shipper without wasting time and resources. You have more time to spend with your family and loved ones instead of spending hours on end jostling with clearing agents.

When we talk about room for growth in this industry, we are not just talking about room for brokers. Once you establish your position in the market, you can also diversify your operation and even start your trucking company. The fact that you understand the freight business better than an outsider gives you an advantage. With the network and resources available to you, it is possible to earn more when you have a registered trucking company. You can start with one truck and, with time, add more to your fleet as the business grows. That being said, you must be careful not to have a conflict of interest when managing the business.

Like most people getting into a new business, one of your concerns is probably the cost of setting up the brokerage business. We outlined the primary cost centers, and once you plan around it, you will realize that you don't need a sizable capital outlay to start. Obtain the necessary licenses, and if you do not have the funds to set up an office, you can work from home. Most of the successful freight brokers you meet in the business started with no more than a desk or working on their dining table at home. With diligence, commitment to the cause and motivation, they went on to grow their operation. As the boss, this business offers you the flexibility to move at your own pace.

If you are thinking about the future, freight brokerage is the right place for you. Success in this business can be the beginning of a huge family business, a legacy that will come for generations. This can be your opportunity to create generational wealth, making your family name one of the industry's household names. What more are you waiting for? Get started and become a freight broker today!

Through your feedback, I am encouraged to write more, which is why I would, as always, love to hear how this book helped you. As writing books is my livelihood, it would mean the world to me if you could write a review with your feedback. With that said, it is time for me to bid you farewell. I wish you the best of luck!

References

Bowen, G. (2018). Trucking company : How to start a trucking company and a freight broker business startup guide. Createspace Independent Publishing Platform.

Burton, T. T. (2016). Global KATA : Success through the Lean Business System Reference Model. Mcgraw-Hill Education.

Debaise, C., & Wall Street Journal (Firm. (2009). The Wall Street Journal complete small business guidebook. Three Rivers Press.

Fliedner, G., & Mathieson, K. (2009). Learning lean: A survey of industry lean Needs. Journal of Education for Business, 84(4), 194–199. **https://doi.org/10.3200/joeb.84.4.194-199**

Guthrie, T. B. (2007). The freight broker's handbook : ten steps to successful brokering. Guthrie Transportation Consultants.

Mccarthy, A. (2017). Freight broker business startup : How to start, run & grow a successful freight brokerage business. Valencia Publishing House, Lexington, Ky.

Mucciolo, L. (1987). Make it yours! : How to own your own business, buy a business, start a business, franchise a business. Wiley.

Серебрянская, Н. А. (2017). Intermodal freight transport models as a strategic direction in the operation of freight forwarding companies. Politechnical Student Journal, 7. https://doi.org/10.18698/2541-8009-2017-2-66